D0720591

Volume Four

Matthew through 1 Thessalonians

From the Bible-teaching ministry of

CHARLES R. SWINDOLL

Chuck graduated in 1963 from Dallas Theological Seminary, where he now serves as the school's fourth president, helping to prepare a new generation of men and women for the ministry. Chuck has served in pastorates in three states: Massachusetts, Texas, and California, including almost twenty-three years at the First Evangelical Free Church in Fullerton, California. His sermon messages have been aired over radio since 1979 as the *Insight for Living* broadcast. A best-selling author, Chuck has written numerous books and booklets on many subjects.

Based on the outlines and transcripts of Chuck's sermons, the study guide text is coauthored by Gary Matlack, a graduate of Texas Tech University and Dallas Theological Seminary, and by Bryce Klabunde, a graduate of Biola University and Dallas Theological Seminary. They also wrote the Living Insights sections.

Editor in Chief:
Cynthia Swindoll

Coauthors of Text:
Gary Matlack
Bryce Klabunde

Senior Editor and Assistant Writer:
Wendy Peterson

Assistant Editor:
Glenda Schlahta

Copy Editors:
Tom Kimber
Marco Salazar

Cover Designer:
Nina Paris

Text Designer:
Gary Lett

Graphics System Administrator:
Bob Haskins

Publishing System Specialist:
Alex Pasieka

Director, Communications Division:
John Norton

Marketing Manager:
Alene Cooper

Production Coordinator:
Don Bernstein

Printer:
Sinclair Printing Company

Series ISBN 0-8499-1474-4—*God's Masterwork: A Concerto in Sixty-Six Movements*

Study guide ISBN 0-8499-8741-5—*Volume Four: Matthew–1 Thessalonians*

COVER IMAGE: *Christ as the Good Shepherd*, stained glass, Superstock

COVER BACKGROUND PHOTO: Superstock

Printed in the United States of America

CONTENTS

INTRODUCTION

The writers of the New Testament used many names, symbols, and analogies to depict Jesus Christ: King of the Jews. Suffering Servant. Son of Man. The eternal Word made flesh. The Good Shepherd. The True Vine. Living Water. Our all in all. Our Righteousness. Head and Sustainer of the Body. Cornerstone. High Priest. The Lamb. King of Kings. Lord of Lords.

Many designations. But while on earth, Jesus had only one mission: to bring sinners near to God the Father through the payment of His own precious blood. For this divine work, the New Testament also has many words: Rebirth. Redemption. Justification. Salvation. Adoption. Substitution. Righteousness. Freedom.

These words blend together like many instruments in a symphony, resulting in one beautiful theme—Jesus Christ, our Lord and Savior.

In volume 4 of *God's Masterwork*, He who was promised in the Old Testament becomes present in the New. Messiah arrives. The little, spotless Lamb emerges as sovereign Lord. May all the words that you read about Him and from Him in these pages be music to your soul.

Chuck Swindoll

Chuck Swindoll

PUTTING TRUTH INTO ACTION

Knowledge apart from application falls short of God's desire for His children. He wants us to apply what we learn so that we will change and grow. This study guide was prepared with these goals in mind. As you go through the following pages, we hope your desire to discover biblical truth will grow as your understanding of God's Word increases and that you will be encouraged to apply what you've learned.

To assist you in your study, we've included a section called **Living Insights** at the end of each lesson. These exercises will challenge you to study further and to think of specific ways to put your discoveries into action.

There are many ways to use this guide—in personal devotions, group studies, discussions with friends and family, and Sunday school classes. And, of course, it's an ideal study aid when you're listening to its corresponding *Insight for Living* radio series.

To benefit most from this study guide, we would encourage you to consider it a spiritual journal. That's why we've included space in the **Living Insights** for recording your thoughts and discoveries. We hope you'll return to those sections often for review and encouragement as you continue to grow in your walk with Christ.

Bryce Klabunde
Coauthor of Text
Author of Living Insights

Gary Matlack
Coauthor of Text
Author of Living Insights

GOD'S MASTERWORK

A Concerto in Sixty-Six Movements

Volume Four

Matthew through 1 Thessalonians

Chapter 1

AN IMPORTANT INTERLUDE

A Look between the Testaments

> "Behold, I am going to send you Elijah the prophet before the coming of the great and terrible day of the Lord. He will restore the hearts of the fathers to their children and the hearts of the children to their fathers, so that I will not come and smite the land with a curse." (Mal. 4:5–6)

With these last verses of the Old Testament, your survey of the Bible is more than half complete. Now it's on to the New Testament, where anticipation becomes actuality. Where Jesus is no longer a mere promise; He's a real, living, breathing person, the Son of God come to live among us. Next stop, the gospel of Matthew!

This is the perfect time to . . . uh . . . slow down, actually. While there's not much paper between Malachi and Matthew in your Bible, there is a lot of history between them—about four hundred years. Knowing how the world changed during that time is crucial to understanding the era in which Jesus lived and ministered.

So before going on to Matthew's biography of our Lord, let's take one chapter to live between the testaments.

The "Silent" Years

Historians have dubbed this four-hundred-year bridge that connects the Old and New Testaments "the silent years," which is somewhat of a misnomer.

Though the period was silent in terms of revelation—no prophet spoke during this time—it was anything but silent in terms of preparation. As author David O'Brien writes, "The events, literature and social forces of these years would shape the world of the [New Testament]."[1]

God's voice was at rest, but His hands were busy building the stage upon which He would deliver His grandest, most eloquent, most moving speech—Jesus Christ, the Word made flesh.

The Rise and Fall of Kingdoms

When Malachi wrote his book, the land of the Jews belonged to the Persian Empire. It remained so until about a century later, when Alexander the Great's military machine rolled eastward across Asia Minor, eventually reaching Palestine and as far as Egypt.

The Ascent of Greece

Alexander dreamed of building a new world bonded together by Greek language and culture. This policy, known as Hellenization, eventually established common or *koine* Greek—the language of the New Testament. Unwittingly, Alexander was a tool in God's hand to prepare the world for the spread of the Gospel.

By 332 B.C. Palestine had been absorbed into the expanding Greek kingdom. History shows that Alexander generally treated the Jews with benevolence, even allowing them a measure of self-rule.

The Division of the Grecian Empire

Alexander the Great died in 323 B.C. at the age of thirty-three. For about the next 150 years, his successors played tug-of-war for control of the empire—with Israel stuck in the middle. One of these successors, Antiochus IV Epiphanes (whose name means "God made manifest"), ruled from 175–164 B.C. An arrogant tyrant, he

> attempted to consolidate his fading empire through a policy of radical Hellenization. While a segment of the Jewish aristocracy had already adopted Greek ways, the majority of Jews were outraged.
>
> Antiochus's atrocities were aimed at the eradication of Jewish religion. He prohibited some of the central elements of Jewish practice, attempted to destroy all copies of the Torah (the Pentateuch) and

1. David O'Brien, "The Time between the Testaments," in *The NIV Study Bible*, ed. Kenneth L. Barker and others (Grand Rapids, Mich.: Zondervan Bible Publishers, 1985), p. 1431.

> required offerings to the Greek god Zeus. His crowning outrage was the erection of a statue of Zeus and the sacrificing of a pig in the Jerusalem temple itself.[2]

Antiochus's blasphemous policies triggered the Maccabean revolt (166–142 B.C.), led by Mattathias, a Jew of priestly lineage, and his five sons. The revolt gained independence for Judah until 63 B.C., when Rome, under General Pompey, dug its iron talons into Palestine. Pompey

> took Jerusalem after a three-month siege of the temple area, massacring priests in the performance of their duties and entering the Most Holy Place. This sacrilege began Roman rule in a way that Jews could neither forgive nor forget.[3]

The Ascent of Rome

Later, in 48 B.C., Pompey lost a power struggle to his former ally, Julius Caesar. Caesar held the reigns of power until 44 B.C., when he was assassinated. Subsequent wars and infighting brought Julius Caesar's adopted son, Octavian, to the throne. Author F. LaGard Smith points out the sovereign hand of God in these historical developments.

> In 27 B.C. the Roman Senate gives Octavian the title of Augustus, and it is this Augustus Caesar who gets credit for founding the Roman Empire with its Pax Romana, or Roman Peace. For the next two centuries the civilized world will enjoy unprecedented peace, prosperity, and, for the most part, good civil government under Roman rule. It causes one to think again of a God who is working through history to achieve his eternal purposes. A century from now one will be able to look back and see what an ideal time this is for the divine events about to happen in Judea, and later throughout the whole empire.[4]

2. O'Brien, "The Time between the Testaments," p. 1431.

3. O'Brien, "The Time between the Testaments," p. 1431.

4. F. LaGard Smith, *The Narrated Bible in Chronological Order* (Eugene, Oreg.: Harvest House Publishers, 1984), p. 1347.

Alexander's kingdom brought cultural and linguistic cohesiveness to a formerly fragmented world. The kingdom of Caesar Augustus ushered in civil organization and peace. But it also brought conflict, for Augustus established the idea that Caesar was a god.

The stage was set, then, for the coming of a greater kingdom —the kingdom of God in the person of Jesus Christ. He would bring to humanity what no earthly ruler could give—forgiveness of sins, eternal life, and the revelation of the One true God.

Literature from the Intertestamental Period

Though no new prophecy was recorded during the intertestamental period, this was still a time of prolific writing. "During these unhappy years of oppression and internal strife," writes David O'Brien, "the Jewish people produced a sizable body of literature that both recorded and addressed their era. Three of the more significant works are the Septuagint, the Apocrypha and the Dead Sea Scrolls."[5]

The Septuagint

Around 250 B.C., the Septuagint (sometimes designated as LXX), the Greek translation of the Old Testament, made the Scriptures available to Jews who no longer spoke their ancestral language, as well as to the entire Greek-speaking world. This translation later became the Bible of the early church.

The Apocrypha

The Apocrypha is a collection of intertestamental writings whose canonicity (being considered inspired Scripture) has been a matter of discussion and debate throughout church history.[6] Today the Apocrypha appears in the Catholic and Eastern Orthodox Bibles but not in the Protestant Bible.

Though Protestants don't consider the books of the Apocrypha the inspired Word of God, there is still value in reading them

> not only for their insight into the national consciousness of Jews in the Dispersion but also for the

5. O'Brien, "The Time between the Testaments," p. 1431.

6. This is not to be confused with the New Testament Apocrypha, which is also noncanonical, written during the first few centuries of the church. It contains stories about Jesus and the disciples that range from the relatively orthodox to the bizarre and fantastic.

> light they shed on the history of the "dark age" between the time of Ezra-Nehemiah and the beginnings of the New Testament and for the background of rabbinic and early Christian thought.[7]

The Dead Sea Scrolls

The Dead Sea Scrolls may be the most significant discovery of manuscripts in modern times. Found in the spring of 1947 by an Arab shepherd who stumbled upon them while searching for a lost goat, these "documents and fragments of documents"

> included OT books, a few books of the Apocrypha, apocalyptic works, pseudepigrapha (books that purport to be the work of ancient heroes of the faith), and a number of books peculiar to the sect that produced them.
>
> Approximately a third of the documents are Biblical, with Psalms, Deuteronomy and Isaiah—the books quoted most often in the NT—occurring most frequently. One of the most remarkable finds was a complete 24-foot-long scroll of Isaiah.
>
> The Scrolls . . . provide copies 1,000 years closer to the originals than were previously known. . . . Of great importance to readers of the Bible is the demonstration of the care with which OT texts were copied, thus providing objective evidence for the general reliability of those texts.[8]

Though God spoke no new Scripture during this period, He still sovereignly preserved and confirmed the Word He had already spoken.

Developments in Jewish Social and Religious Life

When we arrive in the New Testament era, we see new expressions of the Jewish community—such as the synagogues and religious sects—that weren't mentioned in the exilic and postexilic books of the Old Testament. Where did they come from?

7. *The Eerdmans Bible Dictionary*, ed. Allen C. Myers and others (Grand Rapids, Mich.: William B. Eerdmans Publishing Co., 1987), p. 65.

8. O'Brien, "The Time between the Testaments," p. 1432.

Synagogues

The synagogues, many scholars say, evolved during the Babylonian captivity, when the Jews were

> cut off from the temple, divested of nationhood and surrounded by pagan religious practices. . . . Under these circumstances, the exiles turned their religious focus from what they had lost to what they retained—the Torah and the belief that they were God's people. They concentrated on the law rather than nationhood, on personal piety rather than sacramental rectitude, and on prayer as an acceptable replacement for the sacrifices denied to them.
>
> . . . The emphases on personal piety and a relationship with God, which characterized synagogue worship, not only helped preserve Judaism but also prepared the way for the Christian gospel.[9]

Others, such as Merrill Unger, believe the synagogues began in the postexilic era, when the returned exiles sought to supplement worship in the new temple with regular, community-oriented instruction in the Law.[10]

Wherever they originated, the synagogues were well-established by Jesus' day, having become the regular Jewish assembly for prayer and worship. It's no surprise, then, that Jesus went to the synagogues as well as to the temple to teach and heal.

Religious Sects

During the era between the Testaments, a variety of influences splintered Jewish society into religious factions. The three primary groups were the Essenes, the Pharisees, and the Sadducees.

The Essenes were "a small, separatist group that grew out of the conflicts of the Maccabean age."[11] They stressed strict obedience to the Law, similar to the Pharisees. However, they were repulsed by the corruption in the priesthood, so they largely rejected the temple system. They are not mentioned in Scripture, but the community that preserved the Dead Sea Scrolls very likely belonged to this sect.

9. O'Brien, "The Time between the Testaments," p. 1433.

10. Merrill F. Unger, *Unger's Bible Dictionary*, 3d ed. (Chicago, Ill.: Moody Press, 1966), p. 1053.

11. O'Brien, "The Time between the Testaments," p. 1433.

The Pharisees were the party of the synagogue. They were the keepers, copiers, and interpreters of the Law. Unfortunately, they also *re*interpreted the Law. In their vigorous attempts to apply the Law to everyday life, the Pharisees constructed a maze of regulations that came to be known as the Oral Law. Ironically, their man-made traditions obscured the Scripture they so zealously guarded.

The exact origin of the Pharisees is uncertain. In the writings of Josephus, they first appear in connection with the period of Jewish independence under the Maccabees around 135 B.C. Perhaps Pharisaic rigidity grew out of the Jews' desire to preserve their orthodox, spiritual distinctiveness after it had been threatened by pagan leaders such as Antiochus Epiphanes.

Conversely, Greek thinking and culture made inroads into Jewish society through the Sadducees, the party of the temple. This group was

> closely associated with the Greek intellectual movement . . . [and] adopted the Epicurean belief that the soul dies with the body. They do not believe in a resurrection. Somewhat curiously, the Sadducees reject oral tradition and accept only the written law, but they readily apply their Hellenistic logic to their understanding of the Torah.[12]

Though relatively small in size, the aristocratic Sadducees wielded great political power and controlled the high priesthood. "Because of their position, the Sadducees had a vested interest in the status quo."[13]

Into this clashing fray of ideologies stepped Jesus of Nazareth. He dared to challenge the hypocrisy and legalism of the Pharisees and to condemn the snobbery, corruption, and worldliness of the Sadducees. It was a dangerous course to take, and in the end, it cost Him His life . . . but saved ours.

Living Insights

I know. You're champing at the bit to start on Matthew. But here's one more thing you can do before moving on that will help you in your study.

12. Smith, *The Narrated Bible*, p. 1348.

13. O'Brien, "The Time between the Testaments," p. 1433.

It may be a distant memory for you now, but way back in volume 1 of *God's Masterwork*, we presented a summary of the arrangement and content of the whole Bible (Chapter 1: "A Symphony for the Soul"). This is the perfect opportunity to review that chapter and look back on what we've studied in the Old Testament as well as look ahead to what we'll encounter in the New.

In fact, if you want to make it a little more challenging, try filling in the following blanks from memory. If you can complete them without peeking, you may proceed to Matthew, and we promise not to send the Bible police to your home. If you have to peek, well, go ahead. The Bible police will probably pay you a visit, but you can usually placate them with doughnuts, coffee, and a quick recital of the Minor Prophets. Good luck!

The Old Testament

Total number of books in the Old Testament: ______________

Names of "legal" books (5): ______________________________

____

Names of "historical" books (12): _________________________

____

____

Names of "poetical" books (5): ___________________________

____

____

Names of "prophetical" books (17):________________________

____

____

____

____

____

____

The New Testament

Total number of books in the New Testament:______________

Names of "biographical" books (4): ________________________

____

____

Name of "historical" book: ____________________________

Names of "doctrinal" books (21):________________________

____

____

____

____

____

____

Name of "prophetical" book: __________________________

You might want to read the completed list out loud a few times as an aid for memorization. But you also have the right to remain silent.

Chapter 2

MATTHEW: LET'S MEET THE KING

A Survey of Matthew

Our God is a master of irony.

He often garnishes His work with a tinge of heavenly satire—an undeniable, divine fingerprint that makes us smile and say, "God must have been here; who else could have put that together?"

Who else but God, for example, could have even imagined the plan to save humanity by Himself stepping into human flesh? Who else but God would use a flaming star to lead the Magi, who were ancient astronomers, to the One who created the stars? Only God could take a band of Galilean fisherman and make them fishers of men. And who else but God could cause a greedy tax-gatherer named Matthew to leave his earthly possessions behind, follow the Messiah, and give away the riches of His kingdom?

Perhaps one of the greatest ironies of the biblical record, though, is that the long-prophesied King of the Jews came to His people, who should have recognized and worshiped Him but rejected and crucified Him instead. That wasn't the end of the King or His kingdom, however. Jesus Christ rose from the dead, bringing eternal life to all who believe in Him—Jew and Gentile alike.

The gospel according to Matthew is the story of the Great King, the royal Son of David who shed His regal robes and donned the cloak of a commoner so that we could become uncommon—royal children of the Most High God (see also 2 Cor. 8:9).

Characteristics of the Book

Before surveying the book of Matthew, let's compare it to the other gospels to see what makes it unique.

The First of Four Gospels

The gospel of Matthew begins the biographical section of the New Testament, which is made up of the four gospels—Matthew, Mark, Luke, and John. The gospels (from the Greek word meaning "good news") are biographical, but not in the sense that they are

MATTHEW

	Announcement and Arrival of the King	Proclamation and Reception of the King	Opposition and Rejection of the King	Resurrection and Triumph of the King
	Main Emphasis: His Credentials	**Main Emphasis: His Message**	**Main Emphasis: His Suffering and Death**	**Main Emphasis: His Conquest**
	Birth Baptism Temptation	Sermon on the Mount Miracles Discourses Parables	Spread of opposition Preparation of disciples Final predictions Crucifixion	God's power Great Commission
	CHAPTERS 1–4	*CHAPTERS 5–15*	*CHAPTERS 16–27*	*CHAPTER 28*
The King	His identity: Israel's promised King		His destiny: "Crucify Him!"	
The Scope	Teaching the vast multitudes		Teaching the Twelve	
Location	Bethlehem and Nazareth	Ministry in Galilee	Ministry in Judea	
People's Reaction	Increased popularity		Increased hostility	
Main Theme	Jesus is the King, Israel's long-awaited Messiah.			
Key Verses	16:16–19; 28:18–20			

complete accounts of Jesus' life. Rather, the gospel writers selected portions of Jesus' life according to their unique perspectives, which together provide a more deeply comprehensive portrait of Jesus.

But why didn't God just give us one consummate picture of His Son instead of four interdependent views? Because the different gospels were originally written to different audiences with different needs.

Matthew, Mark, and Luke are commonly referred to as the "synoptic" gospels (from the Greek *synoptikos*, meaning "seeing together"), because they are similar to one another in their viewpoint, content, narrative flow, and style. John's gospel is much different. His is the most theological of the four gospels, beginning with Jesus' preexistence in heaven rather than His birth in the manger. In this way and many others, John emphasizes Jesus' deity. John also contains the greatest amount of unique material, while the other gospels have more material in common. The following chart further illustrates the relationship between the four gospels.

	Matthew	**Mark**	**Luke**	**John**
Portrayal of Jesus	Messianic King	Suffering Servant	Son of Man	Son of God
Primary Recipients	Jews	Roman church	Theophilus and all Gentiles	All people
Primary Purpose	Show Jesus as Israel's long-awaited Messiah	Strengthen suffering believers by focusing on suffering yet triumphant Savior	Provide a warm, human portrait of the Savior of the whole world	Encourage belief in the eternal Son of God
Probable Written Order	Second	First	Third	Fourth
Unique Material	42%	7%	59%	92%

The four gospels come first in the New Testament canon, not because they were the first books written (James was probably the first New Testament letter), but because Christ is our foundation.

All the rest—Acts, the Epistles, Revelation—spring from Him. Together, the gospels comprise about 46 percent of the New Testament.

Jewish in Character

Matthew, also called Levi, was a Jew who collected taxes for the Roman government. As such he was despised by his kinspeople. But after becoming a disciple of Jesus Christ, Matthew wanted to give to the Jews instead of take from them. He longed for them to know that Jesus Christ was their Messiah, the anointed King promised in their Scriptures.

He wrote his book, then, with a distinctively Jewish flavor. Matthew showed, more than any other gospel writer, how Jesus fulfilled Old Testament prophecies and was inextricably linked to their whole history. The genealogy in chapter 1, for example, ties Christ all the way back to Abraham and confirms his descendancy from King David. Jesus is continually referred to as the Son of David. The Law is prevalent—Jesus clashes with the Pharisees over its interpretation and application throughout the gospel. Also, Matthew makes no effort to explain Jewish customs, assuming that his readers already understand them (unlike Mark, who takes time to explain them).

As the Jews increasingly rejected their Savior, the Gentiles, in contrast, sought Him out. The Magi came to worship Jesus (2:11), the Roman centurion put his faith in Him (8:5–13), and the Canaanite woman persisted to seek His mercy (15:21–28). These instances and the Lord's commission to "make disciples of all nations" (28:19) all signify that Jesus is the Savior of the Gentiles as well as the Jews.

Teaching-Oriented

Many Bible scholars see the book of Matthew as being constructed around five major discourses:

1. The Sermon on the Mount (chaps. 5–7)
2. The Sending out of the Twelve (chap. 10)
3. Kingdom Parables (chap. 13)
4. Kingdom Living (chap. 18)
5. The Olivet Discourse (chaps. 24–25)

The narrative sections preceding these discourses build up to Jesus' teaching.

The spoken words of Jesus account for about 60 percent of the book's content. Matthew obviously wanted his readers to observe how

Jesus lived but, more importantly, to know and live what He taught. Many commentators believe that Matthew was a skilled teacher in his own right and organized his material for easy memorization. This would have helped the early church hold Jesus' words in their hearts during a time when the possession of books was not commonplace.

Matthew's gospel reminds us that God's inspired Word was given not just to provide us with information but to get into our lives and change us. May it be so as we study Matthew and all of God's Masterwork.

Major Themes in Matthew

Though Jesus' words in Matthew address a number of issues, two prominent ones that rise to the top are (1) the kingdom of heaven and (2) hypocrisy and self-righteousness.

The Kingdom of Heaven

A Jew, in considering Matthew's presentation of Jesus as the Davidic King promised in the Old Testament, would rightly ask, "Where is His kingdom?" After all, the Old Testament so often points to His glorious reign, when He puts everything right on earth, conquers Israel's enemies, and brings about His people's complete restoration.

We need to understand that Jesus' concept of the kingdom has two aspects to it. It is sometimes clearly future (25:31), being fully realized at His Second Coming. But it isn't limited to a future age. In the Sermon on the Mount (chaps. 5–7), for example, Jesus delineates the distinctives of present-day kingdom living. So the kingdom can be "thought of as coming in the person of Jesus (4:17; 12:28)."[1] The kingdom is God's sovereign government, His way of life, that opposes the world's corruption and will ultimately triumph over it.

The word *kingdom* is used fifty times in reference to God's kingdom, and the phrase "the kingdom of heaven" occurs thirty-two times—eleven in parables ("the kingdom of heaven is like . . ."). The concept of the kingdom obviously needed some explaining, both in Jesus' day and in Matthew's, since the Jews were expecting a different kind of king.

1. Leon Morris, *The Gospel according to Matthew* (Grand Rapids, Mich.: William B. Eerdmans Publishing Co., 1992), p. 8.

Hypocrisy and Self-Righteousness

The kingdom of heaven had to intervene because the religion manufactured by the kingdom of the world wasn't producing real righteousness. In fact, it was producing sin.

The curators of this man-made spirituality were the Pharisees, with whom Jesus clashed many times. The Pharisees had obscured God's Law, burying it under a mountain of fastidious formulas, known as the Oral Law, that exalted their own self-righteousness and encumbered those who couldn't keep in step. Jesus' harshest words were reserved for these misguided guides:

> "Woe to you, scribes and Pharisees, hypocrites! For you tithe mint and dill and cummin, and have neglected the weightier provisions of the law: justice and mercy and faithfulness; but these are the things you should have done without neglecting the others. You blind guides, who strain out a gnat and swallow a camel!" (23:23–24; see the rest of the "woes" against the Pharisees in chap. 23)

Jesus had a different message, though, for those straining under the load of Pharisaic legalism.

> "Come to Me, all who are weary and heavy-laden, and I will give you rest. Take My yoke upon you and learn from Me, for I am gentle and humble in heart, and you will find rest for your souls. For My yoke is easy and My burden is light." (11:28–30)

Jesus wasn't saying that He didn't require righteousness from people. As He said in the Sermon on the Mount, "You are to be perfect, as your heavenly Father is perfect" (5:48). This "perfection" or righteousness could only come from a humble heart that recognized its own sinfulness and trusted in God's goodness and mercy rather than pharisaical self-righteousness (compare 5:3). Jesus Himself, not a Pharisaic formula, was the key to the kingdom of heaven. And He still is.

Structural Survey

Now that we have some of the major themes in mind, let's note how Matthew told Jesus' story. This will be far from a detailed exposition, but it will help you set the framework for your personal study of this gospel.

Announcement and Arrival of the King (1:1–4:11)

In just sixteen verses, Matthew takes us from Abraham to Jesus, establishing Him as "the Messiah, the Son of David, the son of Abraham" (1:1). Next, Matthew sets forth two more major themes in the birth and infancy narrative: Jesus' violent rejection by His own people is foreshadowed in Herod's murderous pursuit of Him, while His acceptance by believing Gentiles is prefigured by the Magi's quest and worship. Matthew even links Jesus with Moses through His flight to Egypt and subsequent exodus back to the land of God's promise.

Almost thirty years later, John the Baptizer breaks four hundred years of prophetic silence and prepares the public for Jesus' ministry. After being baptized by John, Jesus receives the Father's public affirmation: "This is My beloved Son, in whom I am well-pleased" (3:17). Afterward, He successfully resists Satan's temptations in the wilderness, establishing Himself as the perfectly obedient and sinless sacrifice for humanity.

Proclamation and Reception of the King (4:12–15:39)

When John the Baptizer is imprisoned by Herod Antipas, Jesus takes up John's message with His own and begins His public ministry, urging His hearers, "Repent, for the kingdom of heaven is at hand" (4:17; see also 3:2).

He immediately begins recruiting disciples and travels "throughout all Galilee, teaching in their synagogues and proclaiming the Gospel of the kingdom, and healing every kind of disease and every kind of sickness among the people" (4:23).

Then Matthew moves into Jesus' first great discourse: the Sermon on the Mount (chaps. 5–7). Here Jesus lays out the standards for kingdom life. He presents kingdom values in the Beatitudes; then He illuminates such topics as genuine righteousness, the true interpretation of God's law, real spirituality, hypocrisy, trust, forgiveness, and good works. The crowds are amazed that He teaches with such authority "and not as their scribes" (7:29). Like a new Moses, He came down from the mountain having given the people a new and deeper law.

Further proving that Jesus had God's authority, Matthew next shows that He can forgive sins and that He speaks for God. Matthew groups together ten miracles that highlight His compassion as well: Jesus cleansing the leper, healing the centurion's servant, healing

Peter's mother-in-law, freeing the demon-possessed and healing the sick crowds, calming the storm, freeing two demon-possessed men, healing a paralyzed man, raising a young girl from the dead, healing the hemorrhaging woman, healing the blind and mute (chaps. 8–9). These miracles "reveal [Jesus'] authority over every realm (disease, demons, death, and nature)."[2]

As representatives of Jesus' authority, the disciples are sent out to preach the Gospel to "the lost sheep of the house of Israel" (10:6). Chapter 10 gives us Jesus' second major discourse, which prepares the Twelve for opposition but also looks ahead to the persecution of the church. As if to emphasize the reality of opposition, Matthew immediately segues in chapter 11 to John the Baptizer's imprisonment, Jesus' judgment on unbelief, and the Pharisees' growing hostility. With rejection becoming more outright and public among the religious leaders, Jesus shifts more attention to His disciples, explaining His kingdom parables only to them (third discourse, chap. 13).

John the Baptizer's execution sounds an ominous tone at this point in Jesus' ministry. And despite His feeding of the five thousand, His walking on water, and feeding four thousand more, the Pharisees' antagonism only increases.

Opposition and Rejection of the King (Chaps. 16–27)

The Pharisees' badgering contrasts sharply with Peter's revelation of Jesus as the Messiah (16:1–20). And Jesus' promise to build His church clearly anticipates the continuation of what He has begun, despite His fast-approaching crucifixion. His transfiguration gives further assurance of the ultimate triumph of His kingdom. His fourth discourse, in fact, lays out some distinctives of life in the kingdom community (chap. 18).

More frequent and intense confrontation with the Pharisees (chap. 23) causes Jesus to prepare His followers for His death and look ahead to His second coming. This is His final discourse, known as the Olivet Discourse (chaps. 24–25). After spending a final Passover meal with His men, Jesus is arrested, paraded through a series of fraudulent trials, and crucified. Mockingly, a sign is placed above his head: "This is Jesus the King of the Jews" (27:37).

2. Bruce Wilkinson and Kenneth Boa, *Talk Thru the Bible*, (Nashville, Tenn.: Thomas Nelson Publishers, 1983), p. 311.

As His lifeless body is placed in a borrowed tomb, it seems as though the King's short reign is over and that His kingdom was only a dream.

Resurrection and Triumph of the King (Chap. 28)

But it wasn't a dream. On the third day, Jesus rises from the dead, just as He said He would, securing salvation for all who trust in Him. Appearing to His disciples in His resurrected body, Jesus commissions them to reach the world with His message. An enormous task. But they wouldn't be doing it alone. Nor will we. For the Baby named Emmanuel, meaning "God with us" (1:23), is now the Risen Lord who proclaims,

> "Lo, I am with you always, even to the end of the age." (28:20b)

Long live the King!

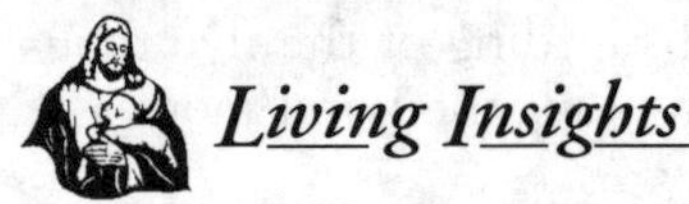

Living Insights

Our Lord Jesus is a sovereign king who rules over all creation. Before His name "every knee will bow, of those who are in heaven and on earth and under the earth" (Phil. 2:10).

That's a lot of power! In the hands of a human king, it would spell disaster. But Jesus never abuses His authority. To do so would be a violation of His perfect goodness. Rather, He uses His power and authority to love, serve, heal, save, and administer perfect justice. Instead of oppressing His subjects, He frees them from the burden of guilt and sin. Instead of hoarding wealth for Himself, He freely gives of His own eternal riches. And His kingdom grows, not through military might or hostile takeovers, but by the power of His message.

What characteristics do you see the King of Kings displaying in the following passages? How is He different from an earthly king? What comfort does Jesus' kingship bring to you?

Matthew 4:23–24 ______________________________

____

____

Matthew 7:7–12 ______________________________________

____

____

Matthew 9:35–36 _____________________________________

____

____

Matthew 11:28–30 ____________________________________

____

____

Matthew 18:1–6 ______________________________________

____

____

Matthew 21:1–14 _____________________________________

____

____

Matthew 25:31–46 ____________________________________

____

____

Matthew 27:11, 35–37 _________________________________

____

____

Now, how about spending some time in prayer, thanking your King for His benevolent reign in your life?

Chapter 3

MARK: THE SERVANT AT WORK

A Survey of Mark

Jesus is our mighty King, yet He is so different from an earthly monarch. The world's kings live in opulence, luxuriating in grand palaces. They issue commands, and their words become law. They snap their fingers, and people jump to do their bidding. They are masters of all, servants of none.

Jesus, however, was master of all *and* servant of all. He has always been the sovereign ruler of creation, yet, in the highest act of humility, He set aside His royal robes, tied a servant's towel around His waist, and tended to the needs of humankind.

People were in darkness, so He enlightened them with His teaching. People were broken and sick, so He healed them. They were hopeless, so He encouraged them. They were in bondage to satanic control, so He liberated them. They were lost in sin, so He forgave them.

He served humanity with a passion that could only flow from a heart full of love. Ultimately, that love led Him to make the greatest sacrifice a servant could make—to give His own life for those He served.

The gospel of Mark captures Jesus' servant spirit in a fast-paced account of His life. The narrative itself reflects the kind of person Jesus was: purposeful, determined, and on the move. You have to wear running shoes to keep up with Jesus in the book of Mark! This was one King who didn't sit on pillows and let people wait on Him; He came to work, to serve, and to save.

A Gospel of Action

One author has titled Mark "The Go Gospel" because events move so quickly.[1] Each one leads immediately into the next. In fact, Mark's favorite word is *immediately*—appearing ten times in the first chapter alone.

1. Manford George Gutzke, *Go Gospel: Daily Devotions and Bible Studies in the Gospel of Mark* (Glendale, Calif.: Gospel Light Publications, Regal Books, 1968).

MARK

	Introduction and Preparation	The Servant at Work	The Servant Rejected . . . Then Exalted
	A brief introduction sets Jesus' ministry in motion.	**An unbroken chain of events reveals Jesus helping people in need.**	**A growing discontent among the authorities leads to Jesus' suffering and death.**
	John the Baptizer prepares the way.	Because people are in darkness, He enlightens.	He presses the claim, "Messiah."
	Jesus is tempted in the wilderness.	Because people are sick/afflicted, He heals.	He spends more time alone with His disciples.
		Because people are without hope, He encourages.	He comes into open conflict with His enemies.
		Because people are in bondage to satanic control, He liberates.	He is hated, deserted, tortured, crucified, and buried.
		Because people are sinful, He forgives.	He is raised bodily from the dead!
	CHAPTER 1:1–13	*CHAPTERS 1:14–8:30*	*CHAPTERS 8:31–16:20*
Emphasis	Service to others		Sacrifice for others
Scope	Ministry to the multitudes		Ministry to the Twelve
Sections	Action . . . reaction . . . confrontation		Revelation . . . crucifixion . . . exaltation!
Main Theme	Jesus is the suffering Servant who gives His life to save the world.		
Key Verse	"For even the Son of Man did not come to be served, but to serve, . . .		. . . and to give His life a ransom for many." (10:45)

Many scholars believe that the gospel of Mark was written in Rome to the Romans, particularly the believers there. Bruce Wilkinson and Kenneth Boa explain that

> this may be why Mark omitted a number of items that would not have been meaningful to Gentiles, such as the genealogy of Christ, fulfilled prophecy, references to the Law, and certain Jewish customs that are found in other gospels. Mark interpreted Aramaic words (3:17; 5:41; 7:34; 15:22) and used a number of Latin terms in place of their Greek equivalents (4:21; 6:27; 12:14, 42; 15:15–16, 39).[2]

For the Romans, a people of action, Mark portrayed Jesus as a man of action, emphasizing His miracles and personal encounters more than His discourses and sermons.

> Only eighteen out of Christ's seventy parables are found in Mark—and some of these are only one sentence in length—but he lists over half of Christ's thirty-five miracles, the highest proportion in the Gospels.[3]

Mark's Source

A word-for-word comparison of Mark with Matthew and Luke reveals an interesting fact: "91 percent of Mark's Gospel is contained in Matthew, while 53 percent of Mark is found in Luke."[4] This has led many to conclude that Mark was written first and that Matthew and Luke used Mark as their principal source. If so, then where did Mark get his information?

From the apostle Peter.

We know this from the writings of the early church fathers. Papias (circa A.D. 60–130) stated that Mark wrote his account of Jesus' life based on Peter's sermons to the Christian community. Justin Martyr (circa A.D. 100–165) even referred to Mark's gospel

2. Bruce Wilkinson and Kenneth Boa, *Talk Thru the Bible* (Nashville, Tenn.: Thomas Nelson Publishers, 1983), p. 320.

3. Wilkinson and Boa, *Talk Thru the Bible*, p. 321.

4. Walter Wessel and William Lane, introduction to Mark, in *The NIV Study Bible*, ed. Kenneth L. Barker and others (Grand Rapids, Mich.: Zondervan Bible Publishers, 1985), p. 1437.

as the "Memoirs of Peter."[5]

In Mark's (and Peter's) gospel, then, you get an intimate, eyewitness description of the inner life of Jesus. William Barclay observes,

> No one tells us so much about the emotions of Jesus as Mark does. Jesus sighed deeply in his spirit (7:34; 8:12). He was moved with compassion (6:34). He marveled at their unbelief (6:6). He was moved with righteous anger (3:5; 8:33; 10:14). Only Mark tells us that when Jesus looked at the rich young ruler he loved him (10:21). Jesus could feel the pangs of hunger (11:12). He could be tired and want to rest (6:31).[6]

Imagine how little we would know about our Lord if it weren't for Mark and his determination to tell Christ's story. And yet, surprisingly, this gospel writer wasn't always so willing to proclaim the Gospel message.

Mark's Background

As a youth, Mark (also known as John Mark) joined Christ's followers and was possibly the "young man" who "escaped naked" when Jesus was arrested (see Mark 14:51–52). His mother, a believer as well, later opened her home to be used as a meeting place for the early church (see Acts 12:12). Mark accompanied Paul and Barnabas on their first missionary journey, but when times got rough, he abandoned the expedition midway through. Paul did not want to give the young man a second chance, but Barnabas (Mark's cousin, Col. 4:10) did. So sharp was the missionaries' disagreement that they parted ways: Paul took Silas one direction, while Barnabas and Mark went another (see Acts 15:36–41).

That's the last we see of Mark for several years. Then, out of the blue, he emerges in Rome, the hotbed of Christian persecution, standing shoulder-to-shoulder with Paul, who is in prison. In his epistles, Paul names Mark as one of his few faithful encouragers and

5. See J. Sidlow Baxter, *Explore the Book*, 5 vols. in 1 (Grand Rapids, Mich.: Zondervan Publishing House, Academie Books, 1960), vol. 5, p. 220.

6. William Barclay, *The Gospel of Mark*, rev. ed., The Daily Study Bible Series, (Philadelphia, Pa.: Westminster Press, 1975), pp. 6–7.

"fellow workers" (see Col. 4:10–11; Philem. 24). And later, at death's door, Paul told Timothy: "Pick up Mark and bring him with you, for he is useful to me for service" (2 Tim. 4:11).

What turned Mark from deserter to friend, from spiritual washout to faithful servant? Certainly, the encouraging hand of Barnabas played a part in his recovery. But it must have been the forgiving arms of Jesus that played the major role. Mark personally experienced the restorative love of Christ, the same love that Mark's mentor, Peter, received after denying Jesus the night of His arrest (see John 21).

Suffering under Nero, the Christians in Rome were teetering over the same dark abyss of denial and defection from which Peter and Mark had risen. The believers needed something—Someone—to hang on to. So the greatest message Mark could give them was the story of the One who had changed his life: Jesus Christ, the Savior who died for them and whose love was worth dying for.

Major Themes in Mark

Mark develops at least three major themes in his gospel.

Discipleship

The first theme is discipleship. When Jesus issued the simple challenge, "Follow Me," Peter and Andrew "left their nets" (1:16–18), James and John "left their father" (vv. 19–20), and Matthew, the tax-collector, left his booth (2:14). Their responses modeled the sort of don't-look-back faith that Jesus was asking for.

In Mark, we learn that true disciples share Jesus' all-consuming purpose: to do the will of God (see 3:35). They set aside their own self-interests and are prepared to lose their lives for His sake (8:34–38). They measure greatness by self-sacrifice and humility, not power and prestige (9:33–37; 10:41–45). And, although they may be called to give up everything, the rich rewards Jesus gives in return far outshine any glittering jewel the world may offer (10:28–31).

The Contrast Between Belief and Unbelief

Second, Mark contrasts the responses to Jesus of belief and unbelief. The people were amazed at Jesus' words: "What is this? A new teaching with authority!" (1:27). Their mouths dropped open when they saw His miracles, "We have never seen anything like this" (2:12). They ran out to greet Him whenever He approached (9:15).

However, while the people clamored for Jesus, the religious leaders fumed over Him. He dined with "sinners" (2:15–17), didn't require His disciples to fast (vv. 18–22), broke prevailing Sabbath customs (2:23–3:6), ignored the leaders' pet traditions (7:1–8), unmasked their hypocrisy (7:9–13), upset their moneymaking schemes (11:15–18), confounded their attempts to discredit Him (11:27–33; 12:13–27), and said they deserved "greater condemnation" for their sins (12:38–40). Rather than repent, though, the jealous leaders demonstrated their hostile unbelief, determining to kill Him and snuff out the Light that was exposing their wickedness (3:6; 11:18).

This leads to the third crucial theme.

The Crucifixion and Resurrection

For ten chapters, Mark steadily builds the tension between Jesus and the Jewish leaders. The inevitable clash takes place in chapters 11 through 16, during the Passover week. Here Mark slows the pace, for this is the focal point of his gospel, the culmination of Jesus' mission, the Crucifixion and Resurrection.[7]

Overview of the Book

The outline of Mark's gospel is best summarized in the following verse:

> "For even the Son of Man did not come to be served,
> but to serve, and to give His life a ransom for many."
> (Mark 10:45)

The first half of Mark highlights Jesus' service to others; the last half focuses on His sacrifice for others. In the first half, Jesus offers a ministry to the multitude; in the last half, He narrows His ministry to His faithful few as He sets His path toward the Cross.

In the very center of the book is Jesus' question to His disciples, "Who do people say that I am?" (8:27). This is the watershed issue of Mark's gospel, the unavoidable dividing line that everyone who examines Jesus' life must face. Who is Jesus? Is He merely a great teacher? Or the Son of God? Our answer inevitably puts us on the side of unbelief or on the side of faith.

7. "Almost 40 percent of this Gospel is devoted to a detailed account of the last eight days of Jesus' life." Wilkinson and Boa, *Talk Thru the Bible*, p. 321.

The Servant Introduced and Prepared (1:1–13)

"The beginning of the gospel of Jesus Christ, the Son of God" (Mark 1:1). Mark establishes Jesus' identity from his first words, confirming it with the Father's words at Jesus' baptism, "You are My beloved Son, in You I am well-pleased" (v. 11). And Mark proves Jesus' identity with His victory over Satan (vv. 12–13).

The Servant at Work (1:14–8:30)

In the chapters that follow, Jesus' acts of service reveal Him as the source of divine power and love. After calling His disciples, He substantiates His divine authority by driving out demons and freeing the satanically oppressed, healing lepers and the crippled and the paralyzed, and confounding the authorities of His day with His wisdom. He calms a storm and stirs one up with His penetrating parables. He raises a girl from the dead and revives the hope of a desperate woman. He reveals God's power by walking on water, and He holds fast to God's truth by standing against the Pharisees.

By the end of chapter 8, however, the nation still hasn't accepted Him as God's Son—even though, ironically, the demons have recognized Him right away (see 1:24, 34; 3:11; 5:7). Some think He is "John the Baptist; and others say Elijah; but others, one of the prophets" (8:28). Sadly, only a few recognize Him as Peter does: "You are the Christ" (v. 29).

The Servant Resisted and Rejected (8:31–15:47)

As soon as Peter voices his confession, Jesus unveils the true nature of His messianic mission—to suffer, be rejected, die, and rise again on the third day (v. 31). From this point forward, the shadow of the Cross looms large over Christ's life. On three more occasions, Jesus refers to His impending suffering (9:11–12, 31; 10:33–34). And the rest of His earthly ministry focuses on those who will carry His message after He is gone.

He teaches His disciples unforgettable lessons about faith. At His Transfiguration, He gives Peter, James, and John a vision of His true glory. When His disciples could not cast out a certain demon, He teaches them about the importance of believing God to do the impossible. He instructs them that greatness is not about being first. He teaches them about divorce, about having the faith of a child, and about the perils of ambition. Then at the right moment, the

Servant-King presents Himself to His people when He enters Jerusalem on the back of a donkey.

During the final week, the chief priests join their rivals, the Pharisees, to get rid of the "troublemaker." They attempt to ensnare Jesus and stir up the crowd against Him, but Jesus snags them on the barbs of their own questions. With the help of Judas, the betrayer, they finally capture the Lamb of God on the night of the Passover. Jesus puts up no resistance. This is the reason He has come, to offer His life as the ultimate servant for the sins of humankind.

The Servant Triumphant and Exalted (16:1–20)

Then, in the quiet of early morning a few days later, His tomb was found empty. He had risen from the dead, triumphing over hypocrisy, injustice, murder—all sin—and death itself! The grace of God has conquered, securing forgiveness of sins and new life for anyone who believes.

Mark's brief account of the Resurrection comes to an abrupt end at verse 8. Many scholars think verses 9–20 were added to Mark's original work because they don't appear in early manuscripts, and the style of writing differs from the rest of the gospel.

However, Mark's theme of belief versus unbelief is once again presented. Despite the women's report that Jesus was alive, the disciples struggled to believe it was true. Not until Jesus appeared in person did they believe.

Mark's message, then, is clear. Jesus is worthy of our faith. We can lean on Him when the stresses of the world bear down on us and we feel like caving in. He is the Christ, the Son of God, the Savior of the world.

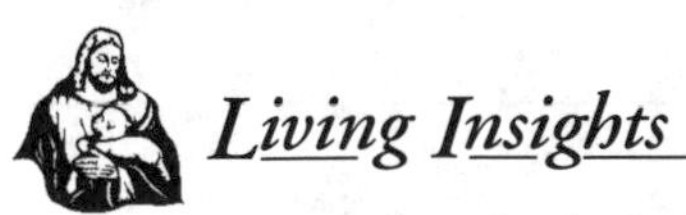

Sometimes our faith feels as solid as an oak tree; nothing can shake our roots. Then there are times when our faith feels as weak as a slender reed. Whipped by the winds of persecution and beaten down by suffering, we can barely lift our heads to pray. Does God love me? Is Jesus who He says He is? Is heaven real?

Christians experience both extremes in life, yet rarely do we hear from those who are struggling. Usually the strong are the ones who tell their stories, while those with doubts and questions sit quietly in the pews, wondering what's wrong with them.

If you've been feeling more like those in the pew than those on the podium lately, keep in mind this fact: The first account of Jesus' life was written by strugglers to strugglers—by Mark and Peter, a former defector and a former denier, to the suffering Christians in Rome.

Perhaps you've never viewed Mark's gospel from that angle before. Try reading these familiar verses from the perspective of times you've suffered hardship and wrestled with defeat and doubt. What special meaning do they hold for you?

Mark 1:9–13 ____

____

Mark 6:45–52 ____

____

Mark 9:1–8 ____

____

Mark 10:28–31 ____

____

Mark 15:22–39 ____

____

Mark 16:1–8 ____

____

Chapter 4

LUKE: THE PHYSICIAN'S OPINION

A Survey of Luke

An American social scientist has observed,

> That the poor are invisible is one of the most important things about them. They are not simply neglected and forgotten as in the old rhetoric of reform; what is much worse, they are not seen.[1]

Jesus sees the poor. And He sees our not seeing.

In the great humanitarian gospel of Luke, the gospel of compassion, Jesus seeks to restore our sight. He wants to give us eyes of love to replace the blindness of indifference. Eyes of truth to replace the distortion of hypocrisy. Eyes of humility to replace the tunnel vision of pride.

For He is the compassionate Son of Man, who came "to seek and to save that which was lost" (Luke 19:10)—both the unseen and the unseeing. He is the Redeemer of the world, the bearer of all human sorrows; and He comes to offer people everywhere God's eternal care through His merciful salvation.

Luke, the Author

Who was this gospel writer who presented Jesus in such human terms? We know Luke was a doctor from Paul's warm comment in Colossians 4:14: "Luke, the beloved physician." Luke is listed here separately from Jews "who are from the circumcision" (v. 11), leading many to believe that he was a Gentile—and making him the

Portions of this chapter have been adapted from "The Doctor Gives a Second Opinion," in the study guide *The Origination of Something Glorious: A Study of Luke 1:1–6:49*, coauthored by Bryce Klabunde, from the Bible-teaching ministry of Charles R. Swindoll (Anaheim, Calif.: Insight for Living, 1994), pp. 1–10.

1. Michael Harrington, *The Other America* (1962); as quoted in *The Columbia Dictionary of Quotations* (New York, N.Y.: Columbia University Press, 1993). From Microsoft Bookshelf © 1987–1994. All rights reserved.

LUKE

The Son of Man . . .

<table>
<tr><th></th><th>Preface</th><th>. . . Announced and Appearing</th><th>. . . Ministering and Serving</th><th>. . . Instructing and Submitting</th><th colspan="2">. . . Resurrected and Commissioning</th></tr>
<tr><td></td><td></td><td>About 90 percent unique to Luke

"Jesus the Nazarene . . . a prophet . . .</td><td>"mighty in deed . . .</td><td>About 60 percent unique to Luke

"and word . . . in the sight of God and all the people." (24:19)</td><td colspan="2"></td></tr>
<tr><td></td><td>CHAPTER 1:1–4</td><td>CHAPTERS 1:5–4:13</td><td>CHAPTERS 4:14–9:50</td><td>CHAPTERS 9:51–23:56</td><td colspan="2">CHAPTER 24</td></tr>
<tr><td>Activity</td><td colspan="2">Coming</td><td colspan="2">Seeking</td><td colspan="2">Saving</td></tr>
<tr><td>Location</td><td colspan="2">Bethlehem, Nazareth, and Judea</td><td>Galilee</td><td>Judea and Perea</td><td colspan="2">Jerusalem</td></tr>
<tr><td>Time</td><td colspan="2">30 years</td><td>1½ years</td><td>6 months</td><td>8 days</td><td>40 days</td></tr>
<tr><td>Main Theme</td><td colspan="6">Jesus is the ideal man who comes to save all humankind—Jew and Gentile alike.</td></tr>
<tr><td>Key Verse</td><td colspan="6">"For the Son of Man has come to seek and to save that which was lost." (19:10)</td></tr>
</table>

only Gentile writer in the Bible. Paul and Luke worked and traveled side by side, and from their first expedition together to Paul's final hours in a Roman dungeon, Luke remained a true friend. "Only Luke is with me," the aging Paul wrote to Timothy from his death cell (2 Tim. 4:11). Clearly, Luke was more than a physician; he was a lover of people, a healer of the soul.

He was humble too. Having also authored Acts, he penned 28 percent of the New Testament, more material than any other writer,[2] and his Greek has been recognized as the finest in the Bible.[3] Yet not once did he include his name in his work. The closest he came was in the "we" sections in Acts, in which he included himself as one of Paul's companions (see Acts 16:10–17; 20:5–21:18; 27:1–28:16).

Luke's Purpose and Style

Why did Luke write his gospel? He clearly stated his reason in the prologue: "so that you may know the exact truth about the things you have been taught" (Luke 1:4). With the care of a physician examining a patient's charts, he studied the accounts of "eyewitnesses and servants of the word" (v. 2), compiled reams of data, and methodically recorded the events of Christ's life "in consecutive order" from the beginning (v. 3).

If you like knowing all the facts, you'll like Luke's style. Compare, for instance, the different ways Mark and Luke introduced John the Baptizer. Mark wrote simply, "John the Baptist appeared in the wilderness" (1:4a). But notice Luke's precision:

> Now in the fifteenth year of the reign of Tiberius Caesar, when Pontius Pilate was governor of Judea, and Herod was tetrarch of Galilee, and his brother Philip was tetrarch of the region of Ituraea and Trachonitis, and Lysanias was tetrarch of Abilene, in the high priesthood of Annas and Caiaphas, the

2. John A. Martin, "Luke," in *The Bible Knowledge Commentary*, New Testament edition, ed. John F. Walvoord and Roy B. Zuck (Wheaton, Ill.: Scripture Press Publications, Victor Books, 1983), p. 199. Luke wrote more material than Paul, if we do not consider Paul the author of Hebrews.

3. W. T. Dayton, "Luke, the gospel of," in *The Zondervan Pictorial Encyclopedia of the Bible*, ed. Merrill C. Tenney (Grand Rapids, Mich.: Zondervan Publishing House, Regency Reference Library, 1976), vol. 3, p. 1000.

word of God came to John, the son of Zacharias, in the wilderness. (Luke 3:1–2)

Luke includes historical details like these throughout his book, as well as medical terms, nautical facts, and episodes from Jesus' life not mentioned in the other gospels.

Luke's Audience

Luke's gospel is addressed to Theophilus, probably a wealthy benefactor who funded Luke's research and published the finished manuscript. However, Luke ultimately had in mind an audience that was much larger than one person. In a broader scope, he wrote to all Christians and, in the broadest scope, the entire Gentile world.

He portrays Jesus less as the Messiah of the Jews and more as the Savior of everyone, regardless of race or nationality. There's a wideness in Luke's gospel—as the angel announced at Jesus' birth: "I bring you good news of great joy which will be for *all the people*" (2:10, emphasis added).

Yet, as commentator Michael Wilcock notes, Luke never loses the individual in the crowd:

> The gospel is not only for Jews, but also for Greeks—and for Romans and for Samaritans too. It is not only for males, but also for females—and not simply important women like the wife of Herod's steward, but widows and cripples and prostitutes as well. It is not only for freemen, but also for slaves—and indeed for all whom society despises: for the poor, the weak, and the outcast, for the thief and the quisling. And all of these Luke delights to show as particular individuals. A galaxy of such portraits glitters across his twenty-four chapters. These are real people, and among them the human condition is really to be found.[4]

4. Michael Wilcock, *The Message of Luke: The Savior of the World* (Downers Grove, Ill.: Inter-Varsity Press, 1979), p. 18.

Luke's Themes and Distinctive Scenes

To portray Jesus, Luke blends themes the way an artist blends colors on a palette. He tints his gospel with such appealing themes as prayer, the Holy Spirit, and praise. He gives a special place to women in Jesus' ministry and deals extensively with the themes of poverty and riches.

However, the foundation for the entire masterpiece is provided by two dominant themes: Jesus' humanity and His love for people.

Jesus' Humanity

Without obscuring Christ's deity, Luke displays His humanity in ways not found in the other gospels. He traces Jesus' human ancestry back to Adam, the first man (3:23–38). He gives us the fullest and most intimate account of Jesus' birth. And Luke is the only writer to unveil Jesus' childhood.

When Jesus begins his public ministry, Luke includes the small but very human detail that He "was about thirty years of age" (3:23). He lets us feel the Savior's heartbeat during His ministry—His zeal "to preach the gospel to the poor," as Isaiah prophesied (4:18), His unrestrained joy over His disciples' success in their ministries (10:17–22), His tenderness toward an old woman whose back is bent (13:10–17).

Jesus' final hours show the deepest and richest shades of His humanity. At Gethsemane, He prays with such agony that "His sweat became like drops of blood, falling down upon the ground" (22:44). His look at Peter after his third denial breaks His disciple's heart (22:61–62). He appeals to the women on His way to Calvary: "'Daughters of Jerusalem, stop weeping for Me, but weep for yourselves and for your children'" (23:28). He offers a prayer of absolution from the cross, "'Father, forgive them; for they do not know what they are doing'" (v. 34). He shows mercy to the penitent thief, "'Truly I say to you, today you shall be with Me in Paradise'" (v. 43).

Jesus enters fully into the human condition. Betrayal, loneliness, humiliation, abuse—He endures it all. Why? Why would the sinless Son of God lower Himself into humanity's dark pit? Why would He let Himself suffer the curse of our sin? Because He loves us.

Jesus' Love for People

To display Christ's love for people, Luke records several moving scenes from Jesus' life that appear nowhere else—scenes like these:

- Raising to life the only son of a heartbroken widow (7:11–15)
- Lifting up a shunned ethnic group in his parable of the Good Samaritan[5] (10:25–37)
- Healing ten lepers on the road to Jerusalem (17:11–19)
- Extending friendship to a despised tax-collector (19:1–10)
- Restoring the ear of the man Peter attacked with his sword when Jesus was arrested (22:51)

By including these vignettes, Luke invites us to come close to Jesus. To feel His tenderness toward the fuming Martha (10:38–42). To experience His forgiveness in the father's embrace of his prodigal son (15:11–32). To see Jesus' devotion in the faithful shepherd searching for the lost sheep (15:1–7) and the frantic woman turning her house upside down to find her lost coin (vv. 8–10). Indeed, Jesus is a loving Savior.

Two Outlines of the Book

There are two ways to outline the book. The key verse of Luke's gospel provides one approach:

> "For the Son of Man has come to seek and to save that which was lost." (19:10)

From the Nativity through Jesus' wilderness temptation (1:1–4:13), the Son of Man *comes*. From Jesus' first public appearance to His ministry in Galilee and final trip to Jerusalem (4:14–21:38), the Son of Man *seeks*. And from the Last Supper through His postresurrection appearances (chaps. 22–24), the Son of Man *saves*.

Another outline emerges from the conversation Jesus has with the two men on the road to Emmaus. He asks them what they're talking about, and they respond:

> "The things about Jesus the Nazarene, who was a prophet mighty in deed and word in the sight of God and all the people, and how the chief priests and our rulers delivered Him up to the sentence of

5. The Samaritans were considered half-Jewish because of their mixed ancestry and were thus deemed unworthy of the kingdom of God.

death, and crucified Him." (24:19b–20)

We will use the structure these verses provide for our brief overview of Luke's gospel.

Jesus the Nazarene Appears (1:1–4:13)

Luke opens his gospel with a brief prologue or dedication to Theophilus. Then he artfully parallels John the Baptizer and Jesus. As Jesus' forerunner, John comes first, so the structure looks like this:

1a) Gabriel's announcement to Zacharias; John's miraculous conception (1:8–24)
1b) Gabriel's announcement to Mary; Jesus' miraculous conception (1:25–38)

2a) John's birth, neighbors and family rejoicing (1:57–58)
2b) Jesus' birth, angels and shepherds rejoicing (2:1–20)

3a) John's ministry of baptism and repentance (3:1–15)
3b) Jesus' baptism and testing in the wilderness, in preparation for His ministry (3:16–22; 4:1–13)

Interspersed in this account are the prophetic songs of Mary and Zacharias, which praise God for remembering His covenant and redeeming His people. Another righteous Jew, Simeon, who was also waiting for "the consolation of Israel" (2:25), prophesied over Jesus and Mary as well. In these devout people the continuity of Old Testament hope is maintained. But they represent only the true remnant, for God's Messiah will soon be opposed by His own people.

Jesus Is "Mighty in Deed" (4:14–9:50)

After His wilderness temptation, Jesus returns to Galilee and launches His ministry "in the power of the Spirit" (4:14). In these chapters, Luke emphasizes Jesus' deeds—His healings, His casting out demons, His initial encounters with the Pharisees, His choosing and training of the Twelve, and His transfiguration. He presents Jesus as having the authority to forgive sins and to speak for God. Jesus' Sermon on the Plain, a more Gentile-focused and social-oriented version of Matthew's more spiritual Sermon on the Mount, is the pinnacle of the authority section (chap. 6). And to reinforce his theme of universal salvation, Luke highlights several Gentile recipients of God's grace: the widow of Zarephath in Elijah's time;

Naaman the leper, whom Elisha cleansed; and Jesus' healing of the centurion's servant.

Jesus Is "Mighty in Word" (9:51–21:38)

Luke 9:51 marks a significant turning point in Jesus' ministry.

> When the days were approaching for His ascension, He was determined [literally, *He set His face*] to go to Jerusalem.

Following His destiny, Jesus turns south toward the Holy City, where the cross awaits Him. Eleven chapters in Luke chronicle Jesus' slow and unrelenting journey (9:51–19:27). This section focuses on Jesus' words and contains a trove of sermons and parables, such as the Good Samaritan, the rich fool, the great banquet, the lost sheep, the prodigal son, the rich man and Lazarus, the persistent widow, and the Pharisee and the tax collector. Here, too, we find Jesus resting with Lazarus, Mary, and Martha; angrily denouncing the Pharisees; and weeping over Jerusalem, which has missed the promised blessings because of rejecting the Messiah.

The narrative builds in anticipation with Jesus' arrival at Jerusalem and the beginning of the Passion Week. His Triumphal Entry, His cleansing of and teaching at the temple, His disputes with the religious leaders, His final words to His followers all lead us to the climax of Luke's gospel.

Jesus Is Crucified and Resurrected (Chaps. 22–24)

Judas' agreement to betray Jesus sets the stage for His ultimate act of mercy, but the Passover supper provides a moment of calm before the crisis. Afterward, Jesus braces Himself in prayer at Gethsemane; then the storm strikes. He is betrayed, arrested, mocked, and beaten. When He is brought before the religious and civic leaders, it takes several trials to convict Him, because it's obvious that they have no real grounds. On three occasions, in fact, Pilate proclaims Him innocent. But the agitated mob cries for His blood, and He is crucified between two thieves with the jeers of His enemies ringing in His ears. What a stark contrast to the praises of the devout at the beginning of Jesus' life.

Jesus' body is taken down from the cross by Joseph of Arimathea, a righteous man "waiting for the kingdom of God" (23:50–51). As Jesus was once wrapped in cloths and laid in a borrowed manger, He is now wrapped in linen cloth and placed in a borrowed tomb.

Thankfully, however, the story does not end here. On the third day, Jesus rises from the dead! The first witnesses to His Resurrection are the faithful women who followed Him. Then He personally appears to two disciples on the road to Emmaus and finally to the rest, whom He commissions and tells to wait in Jerusalem for the coming of the Holy Spirit.

After the disciples watch Jesus ascend into heaven, they return to the city, and the gospel closes where it opened—the temple. But the story still isn't over. In fact, it's really only beginning. Luke's companion volume, the Book of Acts, picks up where the gospel leaves off and traces the spread of Christianity from Jerusalem to Rome. Truly, Jesus is the Savior of the world.

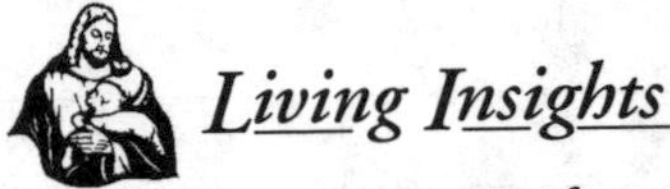

Living Insights

Of the many magnificent themes within Luke's gospel, the most outstanding, according to William Barclay, is this: "Jesus Christ is for all [people] without distinction."[6] Let's use the following categories to acquaint ourselves a little better with Luke's book and get a feel for this great theme. Look up the verses, and jot down the ways in which Jesus expresses His love and concern for all people.

The Samaritans

9:51–56 ____

____

____

10:30–37 ____

____

____

6. William Barclay, *The Gospel of Luke*, rev. ed., The Daily Study Bible Series (Philadelphia, Pa.: Westminster Press, 1975), p. 5.

The Gentiles

4:25–27 ______________________________

____

____

7:1–10 ______________________________

____

____

The Poor

6:20–21 ______________________________

____

____

16:19–31 ______________________________

____

____

21:1–4 ______________________________

____

____

The Outcasts and Sinners

7:36–50 ______________________________

____

____

19:1–10 ______________________________

____

____

23:39–43 ____

____

____

As you reflect on the wideness of Jesus' circle of concern, ask yourself, "What is my attitude toward outsiders?" Are there certain groups or types of people you find difficult to love?

____

____

____

Is there one person to whom you can show Christ's compassion this week? Who is this person? What can you do?

____

____

____

Commit yourself right now to let Christ's love for the lost of this world fill your heart. May the wellspring of your love for others grow deeper with each page of His life that you read.

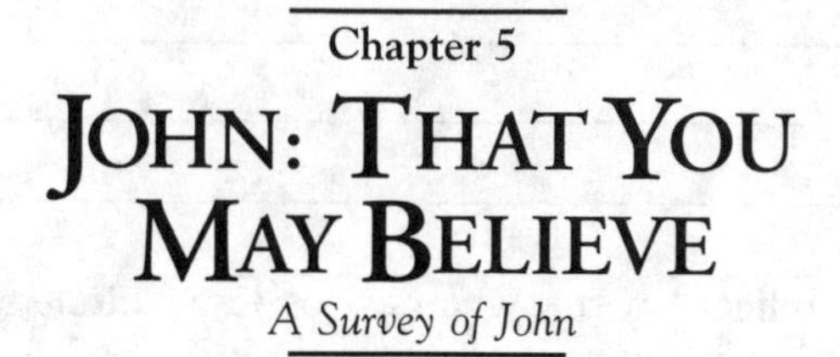

Chapter 5

John: That You May Believe

A Survey of John

How does one describe the book of John in relation to the other three gospels? For centuries, each of the gospels has been depicted by characteristic images: Matthew is a lion, representing the kingliness of Jesus; Mark is an ox, showing the servanthood of Jesus; Luke is a man, revealing the humanity of Christ. And John?

> The *eagle* stands for *John*, because it alone of all living creatures can look straight into the sun and not be dazzled, and John has the most penetrating gaze of all the New Testament writers into the eternal mysteries and the eternal truths and the very mind of God.[1]

John is indeed the most celestial of the four gospels. It begins in heaven, with a glimpse of Christ the Creator before He became Christ the man. But it doesn't stay there; it brings heaven to earth. Because only in Christ's coming to earth could we be forgiven of our sins and brought near to Almighty God.

John the Apostle

John never mentions himself by name, but he places himself in the story as "the disciple whom Jesus loved" (see 13:23; 19:26; 20:2; 21:7, 20; see also v. 24). He was obviously an eyewitness and a disciple. He's also closely associated with Peter, who, along with James and John, made up the "inner circle" of disciples closest to Jesus.

Such details, when considered along with the fourth gospel's stylistic similarity to other letters of John (e.g., 1, 2, and 3 John) and church history's acceptance of John as the author, make it reasonable to conclude that the apostle John, one of Zebedee's sons, wrote this gospel.

1. William Barclay, *The Gospel of John*, rev. ed., The Daily Study Bible Series (Philadelphia, Pa.: Westminster Press, 1975), vol. 1, p. 1.

JOHN

	Deity	God-Man	Ministry	Discourse	Trials and Death	Empty Tomb	Assurance
	"The Word was God." (1:1)	"The Word became flesh." (1:14) *Miraculous signs:* Water into wine (2) Heals official's son (4)	*Miraculous signs:* Heals invalid at Bethesda (5) Feeds 5,000 (6) Walks on water (6) Heals blind man (9) Raises Lazarus (11)	*Private talks:* Servanthood (13) Heaven (14) Abiding (15) Promises (16) Prayer (17)		*Private talks:* Appearances (20)	*Private talks:* Future (21)
	CHAPTER 1:1–13	*CHAPTERS 1:14–4:54*	*CHAPTERS 5–12*	*CHAPTERS 13–17*	*CHAPTERS 18–19*	*CHAPTER 20*	*CHAPTER 21*
							EPILOGUE
Stage	Prologue	Acceptance	Conflict	Preparation	Crucifixion	Triumph	
Audience	Public message		CHANGE	Private message			
Time	Three years			Several days			
Jesus' Seven "I Am" Statements	• "I am the bread of life." (6:35) • "I am the Light of the world." (8:12) • "I am the door." (10:9) • "I am the good shepherd." (10:11)			• "I am the resurrection and the life." (11:25) • "I am the way, and the truth, and the life." (14:6) • "I am the true vine." (15:1)			
Main Theme and Key Verse	"These have been written so that you may believe that Jesus is the Christ, the Son of God; and that believing you may have life in His name." (20:31)						

His book may have been written from the city of Ephesus, where tradition holds that John was bishop, as late as 90 B.C.

Characteristics of John's Gospel

Let's look at some of the characteristics that make John such an important complement to the Synoptic gospels.

Simple Yet Profound

John's gospel has been described as "a pool in which a child may wade and an elephant can swim. It is both simple and profound. It is for the veriest beginner in the faith and for the mature Christian. Its appeal is immediate and never failing."[2]

The book of John is like a piece of fine music. Someone with little or no musical knowledge can still appreciate the beauty and majesty of Handel's *Messiah*. But that same piece is also a technical wonder, studied by musicians who marvel at its breadth, depth, and unity.

Striking analogies (Bread of Life, Living Water), vivid contrasts (light and darkness, belief and unbelief), simple sentence structure, rhythmic flow, and economy of language all make John easy and enjoyable to read. Yet its theological substance provides rich fare for anyone who wants to nourish mind and soul on the deep truths of God. John's gospel is not just a

> life of Christ; it is a powerful argument for the incarnation, a conclusive demonstration that Jesus was, and is, the very heaven-sent Son of God and the only source of eternal life.[3]

Unique Material

Ninety-two percent of the material in John is found only in John—the highest percentage of unique material among the four gospels. John alone records the wedding at Cana, Jesus' discussion with Nicodemus, the Samaritan woman at the well, the raising of Lazarus, and Jesus' washing of the disciples' feet.

2. Leon Morris, *The Gospel according to John*, rev. ed. (Grand Rapids, Mich.: William B. Eerdmans Publishing Co., 1995), p. 3.

3. Bruce B. Barton and others, *Life Application Bible Commentary: John* (Wheaton, Ill.: Tyndale House Publishers, 1993), p. ix.

John also omits material common to all three Synoptics. Absent are the Transfiguration, the parables (John uses analogies), healings of the demoniacs, the new covenant expressed in bread and wine at the Last Supper, and Jesus' agony in Gethsemane.

These differences can be partly explained in that the book of John may have been the last gospel written. The apostle John, knowing about and possibly having access to the Synoptics, may have deliberately written his account to be more complementary than repetitive.

Another reason for the variations is that "John concentrates almost entirely on the ministry of Jesus in and around Jerusalem during the temple feasts. The synoptic writers by contrast concentrate to a great extent on ministry in the north, around Galilee."[4]

The ultimate reason for John's uniqueness is, of course, divine inspiration. The apostle John, though writing in his own style, recorded exactly what God wanted recorded—rich, real images of Jesus and His ministry on our behalf, which would be added to the portrait of Scripture.

Major Themes

What was John's purpose for writing the fourth gospel? Unlike many biblical writers, he told us why: "So that you may believe that Jesus is the Christ, the Son of God; and that believing you may have life in His name" (20:31). How's that for practical theology? John didn't just want his readers to know that Jesus was the Son of God, he wanted them to give their lives to Him, to entrust their eternal security to Him.

It's no surprise, then, that the deity of Christ and belief in Him emerge as two major themes.

The Deity of Christ

Unlike Matthew and Luke, John did not record the birth of Jesus. Rather, he began with Jesus' eternal, preexistent relationship with God the Father. He is the Creator. Sustainer. Eternal source of light and life (1:1–4).

John arranged the events and discourses in his gospel to show his readers that Jesus is the Messiah, God's Son. For example, John's

4. Bruce Milne, *The Message of John: Here Is Your King!*, The Bible Speaks Today Series (Downers Grove, Ill.: InterVarsity Press, 1993), p. 21.

series of miracles, sometimes called the "Book of Signs" (2:1–12:50), emphasize His divine power and divinely appointed role.

Also revealing Christ's deity are the many "I am" statements John weaves throughout the gospel: "'I am the bread of life'" (6:35); "'I am the Light of the world'" (8:12); "'I am'" (v. 58); "'I am the door of the sheep'" (10:7, 9); "'I am the good shepherd'" (vv. 11, 14); "'I am the resurrection and the life'" (11:25); "'I am the way, and the truth, and the life'" (14:6); "'I am the true vine'" (15:1, 5). God used the name "I am" for Himself, remember, when he told Moses how to respond when the Israelites asked who had sent him: "Thus you shall say to the sons of Israel, 'I AM has sent me to you'" (Exod. 3:14). So when Jesus uses the phrase "I am," He's not only telling who sent Him; He's saying that He is God Himself.

Belief in Christ

Only in Jesus Christ, the God-man, can salvation be found. That's why John stresses the need to his readers to believe in Christ.

> The key word in the Gospel of John is "believe" (*pisteuo*), which occurs 98 times. . . . [It] is frequently used in the present tense and in participial forms. Apparently John wanted to stress an active, continuous, and vital trust in Jesus.[5]

Those who "believe in His name" (1:12) become children of God. After turning water to wine in Cana, Jesus' disciples "believed in Him" (2:11). Jesus told Nicodemus that the Son of Man must be lifted up, "so that whoever believes will in Him have eternal life" (3:15). Many Samaritans "believed in Him" after He spoke with the woman at the well (4:39). So did the royal official and his whole household when his son was healed (v. 53), as well as the blind man healed by Jesus (9:38).

Part of John's style in stressing belief is to contrast it with unbelief. "He who believes in Him is not judged; he who does not believe has been judged already" (3:18). Jesus told the Jewish leaders that if they had believed Moses, they would have believed Him (5:46). Not even Jesus' brothers believed in Him (7:5). And the book reaches a climax with the ultimate act of unbelief, the crucifixion.

5. Edwin A. Blum, "John," in *The Bible Knowledge Commentary*, New Testament edition, ed. John F. Walvoord and Roy B. Zuck (Wheaton, Ill.: Scripture Press Publications, Victor Books, 1983), p. 270.

John's message is clear: The only path to life is belief in the Son of God.[6]

Structural Survey

Introduction and Summary (1:1–18)

> In the beginning was the Word, and the Word was with God, and the Word was God. (John 1:1)

What staggering thoughts! Jesus, the eternal One. God Himself. Creator (v. 3). Source of life and light (vv. 4–5). Yet He came to those He created—to recreate them. To bring them His life and light.

In the first eighteen verses, John summarizes Jesus' nature and ministry. He is introduced by John the Baptizer, then rejected by His own people. But to all those who believed, "He gave the right to become children of God" (v. 12).

The Beginning of Jesus' Ministry (1:19–4:54)

"Behold, the Lamb of God who takes away the sin of the world!" (v. 29). These words characterize the testifying role of John the Baptizer. In his short ministry, he introduces Jesus and directs his own disciples to follow Him. John will eventually die at the hands of Herod Antipas, but it is his testifying or witnessing role more than his role as Jesus' forerunner that is highlighted in this gospel.

As John's ministry fades, Jesus' flourishes. He assembles a core group of followers and steps into the social and religious arena. The wedding at Cana (chap. 2) serves as the setting for Jesus' transformation of water into wine. This miracle is the first of seven signs carefully selected by the apostle John out of the many Christ accomplished "in order to build a concise case for His deity."[7] These signs signify a spiritual reality much greater than themselves; the water being turned into wine, for example, points to Jesus' supernatural power to transform—turning a lack into plenty.

6. Life is also "one of the great concepts of this Gospel. The term is found 36 times in John while no other NT book uses it more than 17 times. Life is Christ's gift (10:28), and he, in fact, is 'the life' (14:6)." Leon Morris, note on John 1:4, in *The NIV Study Bible*, ed. Kenneth L. Barker and others (Grand Rapids, Mich.: Zondervan Bible Publishers, 1985), p. 1593.

7. Bruce Wilkinson and Kenneth Boa, *Talk Thru the Bible* (Nashville, Tenn.: Thomas Nelson Publishers, 1983), p. 339.

From Cana, John moves us through Capernaum to Jerusalem and the temple. In angrily clearing the moneychangers out of the temple, Jesus displays His zeal for righteousness. Jesus has arrived as the new, incorruptible temple—where perfect worship, obedience, and sacrifice take place.

Chapters 3 and 4 show Jesus in conversation with two diverse people about the way to eternal life. Nicodemus (chap. 3) is a respected religious leader; the Samaritan woman (chap. 4) is looked down upon by the Jews and lives a promiscuous life. Both take Jesus' words too literally and miss His deeper spiritual meaning (this happens often throughout John's gospel), but Jesus patiently works with them. And His offer of eternal life goes out to both.

The second of the seven signs, Jesus' healing a royal official's son, illumines Jesus' identity as the Word of God—for Jesus heals the boy, who lives in another city, with just His word and His will (4:43–54). The father's belief sets up the coming contrast with unbelief.

Growing Opposition (Chaps. 5–12)

As Jesus' message and miracles seep more deeply into the fabric of Jewish religion, opposition to Him grows. He heals an invalid at the pool of Bethesda (the third sign, 5:1–9) on the Sabbath, which angers the legalistic Jews. And if this doesn't rile them enough, Jesus calls God His Father, making Himself equal with God (vv. 17–18). So the Jews "were seeking all the more to kill Him" (v. 18).

Despite the witness of John the Baptizer, Jesus' miracles, and the truth about Him in the Old Testament, the Jews still refuse to believe in Him (vv. 33–47).

When Jesus feeds a hungry crowd of five thousand from five loaves and two fish (the fourth sign, 6:1–13), the satisfied crowd wants to coronate Him. But He instead turns His attention to strengthening the faith of His disciples by walking on water (the fifth sign, vv. 16–21). When the crowd finds Him on the other side of the lake, Jesus reveals that He is the Bread of Life on whom all hungry souls may feed (vv. 25–65).

As Jesus offers forgiveness to replace legalistic oppression, opinions about Him vary. Some say He's a good man; some say He leads people astray; some call Him a prophet; others accuse Him of having a demon. But everyone, even His enemies, marvel at His teaching (chap. 7).

Contrasting Jesus and the Pharisees, John shows us the Lord's offer of forgiveness extended to the woman caught in adultery—while the Pharisees stand ready to stone her. Conflict with the Pharisees escalates as they refuse to recognize Jesus as the Light of the World sent from God. Then, when He directly states His equality with God ("Before Abraham was, I am"), they pick up stones to kill Him.

Demonstrating that He is indeed the Light of the World, Jesus heals a man blind from birth (the sixth sign, 9:1–7), giving him spiritual sight as well. But the Pharisees, who claim to be all-seeing regarding spiritual things, are the blind ones, says Jesus (v. 41). As He makes it clearer that He is the only way to God, the only Good and true Shepherd, and that the Pharisees are spiritual counterfeits—hired hands who don't really care for the sheep—the religious leaders again prepare to stone Him. But as the hatred of His enemies rises, so does the number of those who believe.

Foreshadowing His own resurrection and depicting the passing from spiritual death into spiritual life, Jesus raises His friend Lazarus from the dead (the seventh sign, chap. 11). This miracle was the last straw for the chief priests and Pharisees. Jealous of Jesus' popularity with the masses and afraid of losing their political security with Rome, they "planned together to kill Him" (11:53).

When Mary anoints Jesus with "very costly perfume of pure nard" and wipes "His feet with her hair," she has unknowingly prepared Him for His burial (12:3, 7). The next day, the humble King enters Jerusalem for the last time, accepting the praises offered Him (vv. 12–19) yet at the same time predicting His own death (vv. 23–36).

Discourse with the Disciples (Chaps. 13–17)

For twelve chapters, John has surveyed the incarnation and public ministry of Jesus. But, as authors Bruce Wilkinson and Kenneth Boa explain, he now

> radically changes the pace in the next five chapters to give a detailed account of a few crucial hours. In this clear and vivid recollection of Jesus' last discourse to His intimate disciples, John captures the Lord's words of comfort and assurance to a group of fearful and confused followers. Jesus knows that in less than twenty-four hours He will be on the cross.

> Therefore, His last words speak of all the resources that will be at the disciples' disposal after His departure.[8]

In one of the most striking pictures of humility in Scripture, the King of Kings stoops to wash His disciples' feet, stressing that loving service to one another is an identifying mark of Christ's followers (13:1–17).

Jesus tells His men that He will send His Spirit, who will bring to mind all that He as taught them (14:26). He urges them to live out what they have learned by abiding in Him, who is the only source of spiritual strength (15:1–11). In this way, they will obey the Lord's command: "Love one another, just as I have loved you" (v. 12; see also vv. 12–17). He also warns them that they will face persecution (15:18–25; 16:1–4), but he encourages them by expressing His love for them and praying for them (chap. 17). For three years He has poured His life into these men. Now His life must be poured out for all humanity.

Arrest, Trial, and Crucifixion (Chaps. 18–19)

Sold out by one of His own disciples, Judas, Jesus is arrested and taken before the High Priests Annas and Caiaphas, as well as Pontius Pilate. Unconvinced of Jesus' guilt, Pilate takes His case before the Jewish people. Egged on by the religious leaders, they cry out for His death, and Pilate acquiesces. In an ironic foreshadowing of the redemption Jesus was about to purchase for all humanity, Barabbas—a robber—is released, and Jesus—the sinless Son of God—is condemned to die on the cross.

So on Golgotha, the sinless Son of God hangs between heaven and earth to bring heaven *to* earth. Creator crucified by His creatures. Son of God momentarily estranged from His Father. The One who knew no sin now suffering for ours. The eternal Word reduced to a few short phrases, spoken in time with agonizing finality: "Woman, behold, your son!" . . . "Behold, your mother!" . . . "I am thirsty." . . . "It is finished!" (19:26, 27, 28, 30).

Resurrection and Reappearance (Chaps. 20–21)

On Sunday, Mary Magdalene comes to the tomb—but the stone has been rolled away; the body is gone. Has He been stolen? Panicked, she brings Peter and John to the empty sepulcher, but they

8. Wilkinson and Boa, *Talk Thru the Bible*, p. 340.

don't understand what has happened either. After they leave, two angels ask Mary why she is weeping; then she turns around and sees Jesus—but doesn't recognize Him. Only when He speaks her name does she understand that He lives again (20:1–18).

Despair turns to hope as the Lord appears to the disciples after rising from the dead (vv. 19–25). Searching Thomas sees His wounds and believes, but Jesus promises that "blessed are they who did not see, and yet believed" (vv. 26–29). And Peter, who denied the Lord three times, is forgiven by Jesus and commissioned to nurture His people (21:15–17). The gospel ends with John's testimony that all he has written is true, and if everything that Jesus did and said was written down, "I suppose even the world itself would not contain the books that would be written" (v. 25).

To find out what happened to John himself, we need to turn to history, which tells us that he was the only apostle to die of old age. What joy he must have felt when he stepped into the presence of the Lord, realizing the full meaning of the words he had written earlier:

> "For God so loved the world, that He gave His only begotten Son, that whoever believes in Him shall not perish, but have eternal life." (John 3:16)

Eternal life. It waits for all who put their faith in the Eternal Son of God.

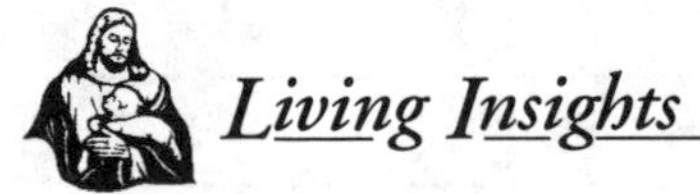

Living Insights

Why is the deity of Christ so crucial to Christianity? Couldn't an ordinary man have died for our sins? Why must we maintain that Jesus is eternal and not created? Why must we insist that He is God?

Simply put, we would have no Savior if Jesus Christ had been less than deity. No one but God could have lived out the Law perfectly, thus earning righteousness for us. And no death but a divine death could have served as adequate punishment for the sins of humanity.

It was not enough for Jesus to be a good teacher or moral example. He had to be God.

Not surprisingly, the deity of Christ is one of the doctrines most often assailed by the cults. For if they take away His deity, they take away His atonement for our sins. Then salvation becomes a matter of our achieving God's favor through our works. And that's exactly what the cults are—systems of righteousness by works.

Why not take some time to look up some key passages on the deity of Christ. You'll not only draw closer to your Savior, you just might be better prepared to share the Gospel the next time Mormons or Jehovah's Witnesses knock on your door. The following references will get you started.

Matthew 1:23 ______________________________

Matthew 12:8 ______________________________

Matthew 26:63–66 ______________________________

Mark 2:1–12 ______________________________

John 1:1–3 ______________________________

John 8:57–58 ______________________________

John 10:30______________________________

John 20:28______________________________

Philippians 2:5–11 ______________________________

Colossian 1:15–20 ______________________________

Titus 2:13______________________________

Hebrews 1:1–4 ______________________________

Chapter 6

ACTS: LIKE A MIGHTY ARMY

A Survey of Acts

Gandhi. Muhammad. Buddha. Jesus. All of history's great religious leaders have achieved a certain degree of immortality—the kind commentator William Barclay calls an immortality of *fame*, for their names have endured the passage of time.

In addition, they've all achieved an immortality of *influence*, for their lives have forever impacted how people think and live. This, too, can be said of Jesus.

But there's a higher category of immortality that Barclay calls an immortality of *presence and power*. Only one Person rises to this level. For "Jesus not only left an immortal name and influence; he is still alive and still active."[1] The bodies of all other religious leaders remain in their graves. Only Jesus' tomb is empty.

The end of the gospels doesn't mean the end of the life of Christ. No, indeed! Jesus still transforms hearts. He still welcomes the outcast. And He still proclaims the day of salvation—through the Spirit-empowered lives of His followers. That, in a nutshell, is the message of Acts.

The Gospels and Acts

The book of Acts picks up where the gospels leave off—with Jesus commissioning His disciples and ascending into heaven. The smoothest transition is between the gospel of Luke and Acts, for the two books have the same author. Eugene Peterson writes,

> Luke continues his narration with hardly a break, a pause perhaps to dip his pen in the inkwell, writing in the same style, using the same vocabulary.[2]

1. William Barclay, *The Acts of the Apostles*, rev. ed., in The Daily Study Bible Series (Philadelphia, Pa.: Westminster Press, 1976), p. 10.

2. Eugene H. Peterson, *The Message* (Colorado Springs, Colo.: NavPress, 1993), p. 237.

ACTS

A.D. 30	The Church Established at "Jerusalem"	The Church Enlarged to "Judea and Samaria"	The Church Expanded to "the Ends of the Earth"	A.D. 60
	The church is . . .	**The Gospel is . . .**	**The witness is . . .**	
	born tested purified strengthened	spreading multiplying changing lives breaking traditions	extended received and rejected changing lives unifying Jews and Gentiles	
	CHAPTERS 1–7	*CHAPTERS 8–12*	*CHAPTERS 13–28*	

Leaders	The apostle Peter		The apostle Paul
Emphasis	Jewish evangelism	Transition	Gentile evangelism
Time	A.D. 30 *(1:1–2:47)*	A.D. 33 *(8:1)* A.D. 37 *(9:32)*	A.D. 47 *(13:1)* A.D. 56 *(21:18)*
Scope	City evangelism	National evangelism	Cross-cultural evangelism
Main Theme	In the power of the Holy Spirit, Jesus' followers carry the Good News of Christ to the world.		
Key Verse	"But you will receive power when the Holy Spirit has come upon you; and you shall be My witnesses both in Jerusalem, and in all Judea and Samaria, and even to the remotest part of the earth." (1:8)		

Luke opens Acts with a reference to his gospel: "The first account I composed, Theophilus, about all that Jesus began to do and teach" (1:1). The key word is *began*. The gospel account was just the first stage of Jesus' life; Acts is the second stage, the second volume of a never-ending story.

In the gospels, Jesus offers His life; in Acts, He offers His power. In the gospels, Jesus plants the seeds of the church; in Acts, the seeds sprout and grow. In the gospels, Jesus is crucified, resurrected, and taken into heaven; in Acts, He sits beside the Father, reigning as the head of the church. In the gospels, the emphasis is on Jesus' earthly ministry; in Acts, the emphasis is on His heavenly ministry, exercised through the Holy Spirit by the apostles.

The Epistles and Acts

Acts provides a rich historical backdrop for the rest of the New Testament. During its thirty-year period (from about A.D. 30 to about A.D. 61), eleven of the twenty-two epistles were written, ten of which bear the signature of Paul. Keeping that in mind as you read the New Testament will add depth to your study. Reading Philippians, for example, will take on a whole new meaning if you first read the background of the Philippian church in Acts 16:11–40.

The Purposes and Themes of Acts

A historian at heart, Luke wrote Acts to preserve an accurate chronicle of the earliest church history. His principal aim was to show the sovereignly directed, Spirit-empowered expansion of the church from Jerusalem to Rome (see Acts 1:8). Under that umbrella objective, we find several other purposes.

To Display Christ's Universal Plan of Salvation

You may recall that in his gospel, Luke portrayed Jesus as the Savior of all people. In Acts, this theme blossoms like a tree in spring, as the good news of salvation spreads throughout the world.

The Gospel message reaches Jews and Samaritans (half-Jews), men and women, lame and poor, rich and noble. Philip witnesses to an Ethiopian eunuch (8:25–40). Saul, a scrupulous Pharisee, becomes God's premier spokesman to the Gentiles (9:1–19). Peter preaches Christ to Cornelius, a Roman (10:17–48). In Antioch, the first Jew-Gentile church is born (11:19–21). They send the first missionaries, and soon, people of every race and religion throughout Asia and Europe are turning to Jesus Christ, the Savior of all.

To Mark the Transition to the New Covenant

Reading Acts, you get the feeling that God is up to something new. For the first time, He pours His Spirit on all believers, not just prophets, judges, and kings. No longer does He require temple sacrifices or circumcision. Nor does He distinguish between "clean" and "unclean" or demand observance of the feasts.

A wind of change seems to blow out of heaven across the pages of Acts. At the beginning, believers worship in synagogues on the Sabbath (Saturday), but toward the end, they worship on Sunday in house churches (see 20:7–8). At the beginning, only Jews come to Christ; but by the end, Gentile believers are the majority. At the beginning, the Holy Spirit guides through the old method of casting lots; but by the end, He speaks through ordinary believers.

We are witnessing the first wobbly steps of life under the new covenant. There were new ways of worship. New doctrines. New perspectives on spirituality. This was a transition time unlike any other in human history, and with changes of this magnitude, conflict was inevitable.

The old-versus-new issue came to a head at the Jerusalem council, when some staunchly Jewish Christians argued that it was necessary to circumcise Gentile believers and "to direct them to observe the Law of Moses" (15:5). The council, however, ruled to accept the Gentiles without imposing the Law on them. What was the basis of their decision? The doctrine of grace and the evidence that God had given the Holy Spirit to the Gentiles just as He had given Him to the Jews (see vv. 7–11). It was a dramatic moment, one that preserved the unity of the church and set the stage for the worldwide proclamation of the Gospel.

To Proclaim and Defend the Gospel

"Jesus is a blasphemer and His followers are heretics." That's what the Jewish leaders were saying about Christianity. Luke wrote Acts to show them that Jesus was the Messiah and that the movement He started was truly of God. Just as no power on earth could keep Jesus in the grave, no amount of persecution could stop the wave of truth that was sweeping across the world. The Jewish leader Gamaliel summed up Luke's message to the Jews:

> "So in the present case, I say to you, stay away from these men and let them alone, for if this plan or action is of men, it will be overthrown; but if it is of God,

> you will not be able to overthrow them; or else you may even be found fighting against God." (5:38–39)

To the Romans, Luke presented Christianity as a legitimate religion that posed no threat to the government. In every case of public disturbance, it was those who *opposed* Christianity who bore the blame. Through the more than twenty sermons and speeches in Acts (most of them by Peter and Paul), the Gospel is proclaimed as a message of grace, freedom, and love.

The Survey of Acts

We can approach Acts from at least three different angles.

Geographically

The first way is to track the spread of Christianity geographically from its flash point in Jerusalem to the farthest perimeter in the world. In Acts 1:8, just before His ascension, Jesus maps out a three-phase course for His disciples to follow:

> "You will receive power when the Holy Spirit has come upon you; and you shall be My witnesses both in Jerusalem, and in all Judea and Samaria, and even to the remotest part of the earth."

The chapters in Acts unfold according to Jesus' master plan:

- Acts 1–7: The events in Jerusalem—God *establishes* the church
- Acts 8–12: The Gospel spreads to Judea and Samaria—God *enlarges* the church
- Acts 13–28: Christianity expands to "the remotest part of the earth"—God *expands* the church

Missions organizations often use this same pattern to guide their outreach strategy: city evangelism (chaps. 1–7), national evangelism (chaps. 8–12), cross-cultural evangelism (chaps. 13–28).

Biographically

We can also tour Acts using the book's two most prominent figures as guides: Peter, in chapters 1–12, and Paul, in chapters 13–28. When we divide the book like this, some fascinating contrasts emerge between the two sections.

Peter	**Paul**
Acts 1–12	*Acts 13–28*
Central location: Jerusalem	Central location: Antioch
Emphasis on Jews	Emphasis on Gentiles
Movement from Jerusalem to Samaria	Movement from Samaria to Rome
Five great persecutions	Four great journeys
Period of refinement	Period of fulfillment

Chronologically

Our third route takes us through five corridors of time marked by certain major events.

1. *From the Ascension to Pentecost (chap. 1).* Jesus' words in the first chapter of Acts provide the momentum for the rest of the book. As He issues His final commands and rises into the clouds, two angels reassure the awestruck disciples that their Lord will return. Comforted, the small band of believers hurries to Jerusalem and waits for the mysterious power Jesus told them would come. And come it does.

2. *From Pentecost to the stoning of Stephen (chaps. 2–7).* On the Jewish holiday of Pentecost, fifty days after Christ's crucifixion, the believers are huddled together in the upper room, when suddenly

> there came from heaven a noise like a violent, rushing wind, and it filled the whole house where they were sitting. And there appeared to them tongues of fire distributing themselves, and they rested on each one of them. (2:2–3)

Filled with the Holy Spirit, Christ's timid lambs rush into the streets like lions, proclaiming Christ's death and resurrection. Miraculously, when they open their mouths to speak, out come languages they have never spoken before. All the people gathered in Jerusalem for Pentecost are able to hear the Good News in their own tongue and, after Peter's first sermon, three thousand people turn to Christ. However, not everyone receives the news gladly. During this period, the early church endures three persecutions:

- Peter and John are imprisoned (chap. 4)
- The apostles are beaten and forbidden to speak of Christ (chap. 5)
- Stephen is stoned to death—the first Christian martyr (chap. 7)

3. *From Stephen's death to Saul's conversion (chaps. 8–9).* Stephen's shocking death sends waves of frightened Christians out of Jerusalem. On their heels is Saul, the fierce young legalist who held the executioners' cloaks at the martyr's stoning (see 7:58). Determined to bring these blaspheming Christians back home in chains, he sets out for Damascus in a murderous rage. On the way, however, Jesus appears to him in a brilliant light, saying, "Saul, Saul, why are you persecuting Me?" (9:4). Blinded and humbled, a changed Saul arrives in Damascus. After a few days, the Lord opens his eyes, showing him a new direction for his life. Saul—later called Paul—will be Christ's principal flame-bearer to the Gentile world.

4. *From Saul's conversion to the missionary journeys (chaps. 10–12).* Although the Lord has accepted and forgiven Saul, the Christians are afraid to open their arms to this former enemy. Compassionate Barnabas, however, extends Saul his friendship, and together they become influential teachers in Antioch.

5. *From the missionary journeys to Paul's imprisonment in Rome (chaps. 13–28).* The remainder of Acts is a travelogue of Paul's four trips: three missionary journeys and his voyage to Rome as a prisoner to stand trial before Caesar. During this period, Paul writes most of his epistles to the churches he has founded along the way.

Here is a brief itinerary of Paul's trips—you may want to follow along with the maps of his journeys in the back of your Bible.

- The first journey: Antioch, Cyprus, Pamphylia, southern Galatia, and back to Antioch (13:1–14:28)
- The second journey: return visits to Syria and Cilicia, Derbe and Lystra in Galatia; on through Asia Minor to Troas; across the Aegean Sea to Macedonia, Athens, and Corinth; and back to Antioch via Jerusalem (15:36–18:22)[3]
- The third journey: from Antioch to Ephesus, Macedonia, Greece, along the coast of Asia Minor, and to Jerusalem (18:23–21:17)[4]

3. During Paul's second journey, he wrote 1 and 2 Thessalonians.

4. During Paul's third journey, he wrote 1 and 2 Corinthians, Galatians, and Romans. (According to some scholars, Paul wrote Galatians earlier, just after his first journey.)

- The trip to Rome: across the Mediterranean Sea to Crete, shipwrecked on Malta, on to Sicily, and finally, Rome (27:1–28:31)[5]

Conclusion

Acts concludes with one of the most thrilling statements in Scripture. Even while under arrest in Rome, Paul kept on

> preaching the kingdom of God and teaching concerning the Lord Jesus Christ with all openness, unhindered. (28:31)

Unhindered. The word unfurls like a banner at the end of Luke's two-volume epic. Nothing can restrain the Gospel, neither threats nor beatings nor prison walls. Just think how far the message of Christ has come, from the announcement of the angels in Luke—"I bring you good news of great joy which will be for all the people . . . a Savior, who is Christ the Lord" (Luke 2:10–11)—to the final cry of an aging missionary at the end of Acts. The messengers may change, but the message endures forever. It is immortal because Jesus Christ is immortal. It—and He—will triumph over all.

Living Insights

Today, resentful people and evil forces still try to shipwreck the church and its Gospel message. In the college classroom, cynical professors take potshots at the traditional beliefs of Christianity. In the media, writers and directors dash biblical values against the rocks of liberalism. And even in the government, politicians seem determined to strip away all traces of Christianity from our society.

Have you felt those forces pounding against your faith? If so, what has been trying to defeat you?

____

____

____

5. While in Rome, Paul penned Ephesians, Philippians, Colossians, and Philemon during his first imprisonment. Later, after Acts was written, Paul was released from prison. He revisited some of his churches, but was arrested again and sentenced to the dreaded Mamertine Prison. From here he wrote his final letters: 1 and 2 Timothy and Titus.

What confidence does the story of Acts give you to face these storms and keep on sharing the kingdom of God "with all openness, unhindered?"

____

____

____

____

____

____

Acts is the only unfinished book of the Bible, for its story is still being written today. How will you appear in its pages? With the Holy Spirit as the author of your life, your faith is bound to make a lasting mark in your world.

Chapter 7

ROMANS: CORNERSTONE OF CHRISTIAN TRUTH

A Survey of Romans

The editors of the *New Geneva Study Bible* describe Romans as

> Paul's fullest, grandest, most comprehensive statement of the gospel. Its compressed declarations of vast truths are like coiled springs—once loosed, they leap through mind and heart to fill one's horizon and shape one's life. John Chrysostom, the fifth century's greatest preacher, had Romans read aloud to him once a week. Augustine, Luther, and Wesley, three supremely significant contributors to the Christian heritage, all came to assured faith through the impact of Romans. All the Reformers saw Romans as the God-given key to understanding all Scripture, since here Paul brings together all the Bible's greatest themes. . . . From the vantage point given by Romans, the whole landscape of the Bible is open to view, and the relation of the parts to the whole becomes plain. The study of Romans is vitally necessary for the spiritual health and insight of the Christian.[1]

Romans has been called a constitution and manifesto for believers, containing the essence and essentials of the Christian life. Though personal in tone, it is a well-developed presentation of grace-filled, God-exalting theology that beckons the mind to stretch, the heart to soar, and the soul to sing.

A Word about the Epistles

With Romans, we enter the section of Scripture known as the

1. *New Geneva Study Bible*, gen. ed. R. C. Sproul, New Testament ed. Moisés Silva (Nashville, Tenn.: Thomas Nelson Publishers, 1995), pp. 1764–65.

ROMANS

THE GOSPEL . . .

Introduction—Personal (1:1–17)

. . . Saving the Sinner

- Depravity of humanity
- Grace of God
- Justification by faith
- Sanctification through the Spirit
- Security of the saint

CHAPTERS 1:18–8:39

. . . Concerning Israel

- Divine sovereignty and human will
- Past, present and future of the nation

CHAPTERS 9–11

. . . Concerning Christian Conduct

- Social
- Civil
- Personal

CHAPTERS 12:1–15:13

Conclusion—Relational (15:14–16:27)

<table>
<tr><th></th><th colspan="20">. . . Saving the Sinner (Chapters 1:18–8:39)</th><th colspan="20">. . . Concerning Israel (Chapters 9–11)</th><th colspan="20">. . . Concerning Christian Conduct (Chapters 12:1–15:13)</th></tr>
<tr><td>Emphasis</td><td colspan="20">Doctrinal</td><td colspan="20">National</td><td colspan="20">Practical</td></tr>
<tr><td>Response</td><td colspan="20">Faith</td><td colspan="20">Hope</td><td colspan="20">Love</td></tr>
<tr><td>Doctrine of God</td><td colspan="15">Wrath</td><td colspan="15">Righteousness</td><td colspan="15">Glory</td><td colspan="15">Grace</td></tr>
<tr><td>Doctrine of Humanity</td><td colspan="12">Fallen</td><td colspan="12">Dead</td><td colspan="12">Saved</td><td colspan="12">Struggling</td><td colspan="12">Freed</td></tr>
<tr><td>Doctrine of Sin</td><td colspan="15">Exposed</td><td colspan="15">Conquered</td><td colspan="15">Explained</td><td colspan="15">Forgiven</td></tr>
<tr><td>Scope</td><td colspan="15">Dead in sin</td><td colspan="15">Dead to sin</td><td colspan="15">Peace with God</td><td colspan="15">Love for others</td></tr>
<tr><td>Main Theme</td><td colspan="60">God’s righteousness is given to those who put their faith in Jesus Christ.</td></tr>
<tr><td>Key Verses</td><td colspan="60">1:16–17</td></tr>
</table>

Epistles or the letters. These writings, Romans through Jude, expand on the truths about Christ presented in the gospels and Acts and set forth the implications and outworkings of the Christian life. They also deal with a variety of issues critical to the life of the church—doctrinal purity, organization and implementation of worship, relationships within and outside the church, suffering, persecution, and so on.

Of the twenty-one epistles, Paul wrote thirteen. John wrote three, Peter wrote two, and James and Jude wrote one apiece. No one knows for sure who wrote Hebrews, although many scholars suggest it could very well be Paul's fourteenth letter.

Background of Romans

Paul did not establish the church in Rome, nor had he visited it at the time of his letter, though he was well aware of its growth and impact (Rom. 1:8–13). It's likely that this church began shortly after Pentecost (see Acts 2), as Roman Jews returned from Jerusalem to their city with the fire of the Gospel still burning in their hearts. The Good News then spread to Rome's vast Gentile population.

Concurrent with the Roman church's growth was the success of Paul's missionary efforts to the east. By the time Paul wrote to the Romans, he had been evangelizing, planting churches, and training leaders from Judea to Macedonia for about ten years. The time had come for him to take the Gospel to new territories.

So he set his sights on Spain. From the city of Corinth, he planned to deliver a monetary gift to the church in Jerusalem, given by the Gentile churches in Achaia and Macedonia. Then he would sail from Jerusalem to Spain, stopping at Rome, the capital of the Empire, to encourage the Christians there in their walk with Christ.

In Corinth, probably in the winter of A.D. 57, Paul dictated a letter to his personal scribe, Tertius, telling the Roman Christians about his plans. But this letter is no mere itinerary. Paul saw his correspondence as an opportunity to ground the Romans in the essentials of the faith, for the church there had no definitive statement of Christian truth. They needed a "constitution" to go by, not just so they could learn, but so they could be a light to the rest of the Empire.

Survey of Romans

The letter unfolds in a logical, polemical fashion, as Paul argues his case that God provides for us what He requires of us—perfect righteousness. Through faith in Christ alone, a "righteousness from God" is granted to sinners, which removes God's holy wrath toward us and brings us into loving relationship with Him forever.

Introduction (1:1–17)

Paul opens his letter by identifying himself as "a bond-servant of Christ Jesus, called as an apostle, set apart for the gospel of God" (1:1). Now there's a man who knew himself, his God, and his mission, which was to preach the Gospel—for the Gospel is the "power of God for salvation to everyone who believes" (v. 16).

Next Paul introduces his main theme, the "righteousness of God" (v. 17), which he develops throughout the letter. The term *righteousness*, which appears thirty-five times in this book, is defined by Paul as inward and outward conformity to God's Law. And no one, he contends, can attain righteousness apart from divine intervention. The righteousness we need in order to please God must come from God Himself.

The Bad News: We're All Guilty (1:18–3:20)

Why must righteousness be a gift from God? Because all humanity is *un*righteous, corrupted by sin and unable to live according to God's perfect standards.

Though some people live better lives than others, at least from a human perspective, everyone is guilty before God—we've all missed the mark: "There is none righteous, not even one" (v. 10). The whole of sinful humanity is in the crosshairs of God's judgment.

Pretty bleak picture, isn't it? If we stopped here, we would be doomed to despair and destruction. But there's more to the story.

The Good News: God Has Given Us His Righteousness (3:21–5:21)

How could sinful people possibly appease the wrath of God? We can't. So God Himself provided the way, through the death of His Son on the cross. Though we have all "sinned and fall[en] short of the glory of God" (v. 23), we can be "justified as a gift by His grace through the redemption which is in Christ Jesus" (v. 24).

Just what does "justification" mean? Does it mean that, by

accepting Christ's offer of salvation, we are made instantly righteous? No. It means we are *declared* righteous. We can enjoy a relationship with God as though we were righteous, even though we will spend all our years on earth working to get our day-to-day lives to catch up with our position.

Righteousness without works? Paul anticipates that his Jewish readers might struggle with this idea. Rituals, after all, played a major part in Jewish religion. Some of the Jews coming to Christ wanted to maintain that certain rites, such as circumcision, were a necessary component of salvation.

Yet Jewish history is filled with examples of justification by faith alone, and Paul is quick to bring them to light. First, Abraham, the father of the Jews, whose belief was "credited to him as righteousness" *before* he was circumcised (4:3). And next, David, whose sins were *not* credited to his account, though they certainly warranted God's wrath (vv. 7–9).

In 2 Corinthians, Paul puts it this way: "He made Him who knew no sin to be sin on our behalf, so that we might become the righteousness of God in Him" (2 Cor. 5:21).

That is truly good news! For Jew and Gentile, circumcised and uncircumcised alike.

Just as Adam's disobedience brought sin and death to humanity, Christ's obedience brings righteousness and life (Rom. 5:18–19).

More Good News: We Don't Have to Live As We Used To (Chaps. 6–8)

Staying one step ahead of his readers, Paul anticipates the inevitable question.

> What shall we say then? Are we to continue in sin so that grace may increase? (6:1)

In other words, since we're justified and will remain so even if we sin, can't we just live however we want? "May it never be!" exclaims Paul. "How shall we who died to sin still live in it?" (v. 2).

Salvation doesn't free us to sin; it frees us to *not* sin (vv. 2–11). As believers in Christ, we are united with Christ Himself and His strength. Sin no longer has a claim on our lives. We're "alive to God in Christ Jesus" (v. 11).

The daily process of living this new life in Christ is called "sanctification" (see v. 22). Whereas justification is God's *declaration* of righteousness, sanctification is our *development* in righteousness.

Justification has to do with our *position* in Christ. Sanctification is the *process* of becoming more like Christ.

As growing Christians, we no longer live under the Law, which showed us our sin and condemned us. Instead we live in the Spirit, who frees us to love and serve Christ.

Old habits die hard, though, as we all know. Even though we're new creatures in Christ and will one day be perfect, we retain the vestiges of our old, sinful nature in this life (chap. 7). This war of the two natures is a struggle for the Christian who truly wants to grow.

But even in the midst of the struggle, the Spirit who dwells within us gives assurance that we are children of God who will one day stand in His presence (8:16–18). We will one day be free from all sin and suffering (vv. 23–25). The Spirit even helps us pray when we can't find the words (vv. 26–27).

The Spirit is our source of strength but also a sign of our security in Christ. Security that God works for our good (v. 28). Security that we were chosen by God and will one day see Him face-to-face (vv. 29–30). Security that God is for us and not against us (v. 31). And security that nothing, either in heaven or on earth, can separate us from the love of God (vv. 38–39).

The Future of Israel (Chaps. 9–11)

Not everyone, however, has that sense of security; not everyone is saved. And that grieved Paul, especially since many of the unsaved were fellow Jews. How could it be that God's covenant people of old could be so resistant to the Gospel?

Paul explains that Israel's rejection of God is both a matter of God's sovereign choice (chap. 9) and Israel's stubbornness and self-righteousness (chap. 10).

Does that mean God has given up on Israel? Paul's vivid depiction of an olive tree in chapter 11 assures us that He hasn't. Though unbelieving Jews have been "cut off" from the olive tree (the community of the redeemed) and believing Gentiles have been grafted in, "all Israel" (11:26) will one day be saved and grafted back in.

This divine plan causes Paul to praise God for His "unfathomable ways" (v. 33). Though we can't always explain why God does things the way He does them, we can trust that He is God. And His plans, like His person, are perfect.

How, Then, Are We to Live? (12:1–15:13)

Having laid out the truth of what Christ has done for us, Paul, in his usual style, now turns his attention to how life changes for those who are in Christ.

In light of the "mercies of God" (chapters 1–11), Paul urges us to

> present [our] bodies a living and holy sacrifice, acceptable to God, which is [our] spiritual service of worship. (12:1)

What does this mean? It means that the Christian life is a sacrificial offering of gratitude to the God who has set us free to serve Him.

How do we serve Him? Rather than being "conformed" to the world, we're to be "transformed by the renewing of" our minds (v. 2). And rather than dwelling on our own importance, we're to consider the value of others (vv. 3–8). We're to live in a way that serves and benefits others, and combat evil with good (vv. 9–21).

The realm of civil government also takes on new meaning for the Christian. We're to pray for our leaders, submit to them, and live exemplary lives under their reign (chap. 13).

Life in Christ also brings freedom from external standards of righteousness. Though we're all to be sensitive to and respect the convictions held by others, righteousness isn't defined by our participation or abstinence. "The kingdom of God," says Paul, "is not eating and drinking, but righteousness and peace and joy in the Holy Spirit" (14:17).

Pleasing ourselves isn't the goal of the Christian life (15:1). We're to follow the example of Christ and work for the good of our neighbor, "accept[ing] one another, just as Christ also accepted us to the glory of God" (v. 7).

The Christian life is a different life. And all the resources we need to live it are found in Christ Himself.

Conclusion (15:14–16:27)

With the lesson now complete, Paul finishes his letter on a more personal note. Commentator John Stott captures the essence of Paul's heartfelt conclusion.

> The apostle seems to be experiencing a twinge of apprehension about how his letter will be received. If so, the rest of it will disarm and reassure them. He writes very personally (maintaining an "I–you" directness throughout), affectionately ("my brothers," 15:14)

> and candidly. He opens his heart to them about the past, present and future of his ministry, he asks humbly for their prayers, and he sends them many greetings. In these ways he gives us insight into the outworking of God's providence in his life and work.[2]

Paul closes his letter in a way we would expect from a man who simply couldn't get over the grace and the greatness of God.

> To the only wise God, through Jesus Christ, be the glory forever. Amen. (16:27)

We don't know for sure whether Paul ever made it to Spain. But he did eventually travel to Rome—as a prisoner—and ministered there under house arrest for two years (see Acts 28:16–31). His second journey to Rome ended in martyrdom in A.D. 68. The Emperor Nero's execution order ended the apostle's life, but it couldn't silence his voice.

And it never will.

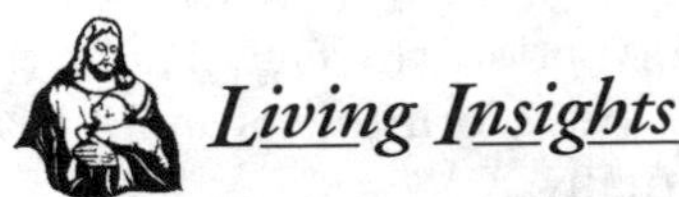

Living Insights

Do you ever feel unprepared when opportunities arise to tell a friend or neighbor about Jesus Christ? Well, you need look no further than Romans for an organized, thoughtful, and clear presentation of the Gospel.

Romans tells us, first of all, that all humanity is guilty before God and in danger of His judgment (1:18–3:20). It also tells us that we can be made righteous in God's sight by trusting in Christ alone for salvation (3:21–31). After we're saved, we are at peace with God. We become His children and live a new life of freedom in Christ (6–8).

That's the good news in a nutshell. Why not take some time to reread Romans 1–8 and pick out some key verses along the way— for example, Romans 3:23, "for all have sinned and fall short of the glory of God," sums up the sin section—that will serve as an outline for your sharing the Gospel with a friend.

Keep these verses handy or even commit them to memory for the next opportunity you have to share the good news.

2. John Stott, *Romans: God's* Good News *for the World* (Downers Grove, Ill.: InterVarsity Press, 1994), p. 377.

Chapter 8

1 CORINTHIANS: CONFLICTS AT CHURCH

A Survey of 1 Corinthians

If you ever find the perfect church, don't join it; you'll ruin it."

These words of advice, given by a seminary professor to a room full of aspiring young pastors, remind us that looking for a church without problems makes about as much sense as shopping for a car that will never need maintenance. On this side of heaven, where we live in a world tainted by sin, the work of holiness is an ongoing project—even in the best of churches.

It has always been that way. Wherever and whenever the Gospel has borne fruit, Satan has tried to spoil it. Not even the church in Corinth, with all its affluence, giftedness, and exposure to apostolic teaching, was immune to worldly corruption. In fact, Paul, who founded the church, had to write to the Corinthians more than once to get them back on track spiritually.

First Corinthians provides a challenge—and hope—for a people in process. A challenge to reflect a perfect Savior in the way we live, even though we are imperfect. And the certain hope that our struggle will one day be over, and we will stand perfected in the presence of our Savior.

Background of 1 Corinthians

Before opening Paul's letter, let's learn a little bit about the city of Corinth and Paul's connection with the church there.

The City of Corinth

Corinth, estimated population 700,000, was a city of supreme importance and notoriety in Paul's day—a "bustling hub of worldwide commerce, degraded culture, and idolatrous religion."[1]

Due west of Athens, Corinth stood like a sentry on the narrow isthmus connecting central and southern Greece. Its location made

1. Bruce Wilkinson and Kenneth Boa, *Talk Thru the Bible* (Nashville, Tenn.: Thomas Nelson Publishers, 1983), p. 381.

1 CORINTHIANS

	Introduction (1:1–9)	Rebuke for Sinful Conditions		Reply to Specific Questions	Conclusion (16:10–24)
		Divisions in the Church	**Disorders in the Church**	**Difficulties in the Church**	
		Exposition (1:10–17) Explanation (1:18–4:5) Exhortation (4:6–21)	Moral disorder (5:1–13) Legal disorder (6:1–11) Carnal disorder (6:12–20)	Domestic difficulty—marriage and divorce (7:1–40) Social difficulty—liberty and license (8:1–11:1) Ecclesiastical difficulty—women and worship (11:2–34) Practical difficulty—gifts and body (12:1–14:40) Doctrinal difficulty—death and resurrection (15:1–58) Financial difficulty—giving and receiving (16:1–9)	
		CHAPTERS 1:10–4:21	*CHAPTERS 5–6*	*CHAPTERS 7:1–16:9*	
Key		“I exhort you . . .” (1:10)		“Now concerning the things about which you wrote . . .” (7:1)	
Need		Unity among the Corinthian Christians		Clarity regarding six areas of concern	
Main Theme		Christian conduct in the local church			
Key Verses		6:9–11; 13			

it a premier center of commerce and trade. With its two huge harbors, Corinth was a frequent stop for ships traveling east and west across the Mediterranean. Many sailors, in order to avoid the arduous 200-mile journey around southern Greece, paid to have their ships and cargo transported across the four-mile-wide isthmus.

Such flourishing trade, along with the protection of Rome's military machine (Corinth was a Roman colony) and the attraction of the Isthmian Games (second only to the Olympian Games), made Corinth a prosperous city. And with prosperity came all the attending pleasures and perversions.

"Pleasure-seekers," write authors Bruce Wilkinson and Kenneth Boa, "came there to spend money on a holiday from morality. Corinth became so notorious for its evils that the term *Korinthiazomai* ('to act like a Corinthian') became a synonym for debauchery and prostitution."[2]

Shrines and temples to the gods were everywhere, the most renowned being the Temple of Aphrodite, the goddess of love. It stood atop an 1,800-foot precipice and employed hundreds of cult prostitutes who helped "worshipers" pay tribute to the goddess.

The Apostle Paul and the Corinthians

Into this haven of paganism stepped the apostle Paul with the Gospel message in A.D. 51—during his second missionary journey. There he met Priscilla and Aquila and joined them in their trade of tent-making to support himself (see Acts 18). When Silas and Timothy arrived in Corinth, bringing a monetary gift from Philippi, the apostle began to devote all his time to preaching the Gospel.

After teaching in Corinth for eighteen months, Paul departed for Jerusalem, stopping along the way in Ephesus. Priscilla and Aquila accompanied Paul to Ephesus and remained there to train Apollos, who eventually went to Corinth to teach the church there.

After this, Paul had several correspondences with the Corinthian church, probably four. But only two, 1 and 2 Corinthians, have been preserved. We know 1 Corinthians wasn't the first letter Paul wrote to them, since that letter refers to an earlier correspondence (1 Cor. 5:9–11).

First Corinthians was probably written from Ephesus during Paul's third missionary journey, around A.D. 54 or 55. Several problems within the Corinthian church had been reported to Paul, and

2. Wilkinson and Boa, *Talk Thru the Bible*, p. 381.

the members there had posed several theological questions to the apostle. In 1 Corinthians, he aimed to address both the problems and the questions, as well as help his brothers and sisters in Christ live out the light of the Gospel in a pagan society.

Structure of 1 Corinthians

The letter falls into two main sections: rebuke for sinful conditions (chaps. 1–6) and reply to specific questions (chaps. 7–16). Within this overall framework, Paul addresses divisions, disorders, and difficulties in the Corinthian church.

Divisions in the Church (Chaps. 1–4)

In the first few lines of his letter (1:1–9), Paul begins his model for confronting difficult issues in the church. Before he ever mentions the problems, Paul affirms the Corinthians' calling as saints in Christ, expresses his thankfulness for their salvation and giftedness, and exalts the faithfulness of God.

Having established his love for them, he's now ready to admonish them. News has reached Paul through Chloe, apparently a member of the Corinthian church, that factions have developed in the church according to the popularity of certain teachers, of which Paul is one (v. 12). People are feeling proud about the teachers they follow.

Paul quickly turns the discussion to Christ and the Cross (vv. 13–17). Realizing that distraction from the Gospel underlies the Corinthians' disunity, Paul sets out to explain that Christ and His wisdom, not human wisdom, is responsible for their salvation. Therefore, they are to "boast in the Lord" alone (v. 31).

Paul discouraged people-worship. Despite his popularity among Christians, and particularly among the Corinthians, he "determined to know nothing among [them] except Jesus Christ, and Him crucified" (2:2). The strength of his message did not reside in persuasive words but in the "demonstration of the Spirit and of power" (v. 4). In fact, it is the Holy Spirit, not human teachers, who enlightens people and brings them to faith (vv. 11–16).

The Corinthians' clamoring after certain men reveals their spiritual immaturity (3:1–4). Paul, Apollos, Peter, and other gifted teachers were merely being used by God to impact the Corinthians at various levels of spiritual growth (vv. 5–9). All Christians are connected to God through Christ. He is our thread of spiritual commonality, not human leaders (vv. 21–23), and we are all His servants (4:1).

The Corinthians have become arrogant (v. 6). They have put too much importance on human strength and appearance; they even have a twisted idea of what it means to be an apostle. But Paul reminds them that we should delight in human weakness, rather than puff up with pride. For when we are weak, Christ is strong (vv. 8–21).

Disorder in the Church (Chaps. 5–6)

Following people, however, wasn't the Corinthians' only problem. They were also led around by their own passions, which caused moral disorder in the church. One member of the church was having an affair with his stepmother (5:1). Instead of confronting the man with his sin, the Corinthians permitted the relationship to continue.

Paul compares the refusal to deal with this sin to leaven, which corrupts the "whole loaf" (the church). In order to protect the church from further sin, Paul commands them to "remove the wicked man from among yourselves" (v. 13).

The Corinthians had drifted so far back into the pagan lifestyle that they were even suing one another in city courts instead of arbitrating cases themselves (6:1–8). The Corinthians were behaving like they used to behave before Christ "washed" them clean (vv. 9–11).

"All things are lawful for me" (v. 12) "had apparently become a slogan to cloak the immorality of some in Corinth."[3] Although the Corinthians were indeed free in Christ to enjoy life, they were taking advantage of their freedom. Many were apparently still engaging in sexual immorality, "joining" themselves with prostitutes (v. 16) and thus hindering their union with Christ.

Paul's command to them, and to us, is a simple one: "Flee immorality. . . . For you have been bought with a price: therefore glorify God in your body" (vv. 18, 20).

3. David K. Lowery, "1 Corinthians," in *The Bible Knowledge Commentary*, New Testament edition, ed. John F. Walvoord and Roy B. Zuck (Wheaton, Ill.: Scripture Press Publications, Victor Books, 1983), p. 516.

Difficulties in the Church (7:1–16:9)

In the letter's largest section, Paul addresses several topics about which the Corinthians had inquired. Each of these practical issues has at its center the desire to honor Christ by bringing every area of the new life under His control.

Marriage

Regarding marriage, Paul confirms that celibacy is desirable. But if a man and woman marry, they should fulfill their obligations to satisfy each other sexually (7:3–4). Christian couples should not divorce (vv. 10–11). Even Christians who are now married to non-believers should stay in the marriage if possible, as a "sanctifying" influence in the relationship (v. 14). If, however, the unbelieving spouse leaves the believing spouse, the Christian is not bound to keep the relationship together (v. 15).

"Wherever you find yourself—single, married, circumcised, uncircumcised, slave or free—honor Christ where you are." That could be Paul's advice in summary. It's not that we have to change our status in life as much as we should see that status as a sphere of influence for Christ (vv. 17–24).

Paul, though high on marriage, also points out the advantages of remaining single. Single people could undistractedly devote their lives to the Lord's work without fear of submitting their families to persecution (vv. 25–35).

Eating Meat Sacrificed to Idols

Concerning the eating of meat sacrificed to idols (chap. 8), Paul explains that some will be able to do this without being troubled in conscience—that's Christian liberty. But others, having been saved out of a background of idol-worship, may be troubled by this practice. In that case, says Paul, we should be willing to limit our liberties so as not to cause a "brother to stumble" (v. 13).

Paul used his own life as an example of the benefits of voluntarily limiting personal liberty (chap. 9). Though Paul and his co-workers had every right to eat, drink, marry, and collect funds for their work of preaching the Gospel, they pursued none of these things. Preaching the Gospel was its own reward. Though "free from all men," Paul made himself "a slave to all, so that I may win more" (v. 19).

The Corinthians may have felt privileged because they had been chosen and saved by God. And they were. But they had wrongly assumed that God would not discipline them if they took their Christian liberty to extremes. In chapter 10, Paul uses the example of the Old Testament Israelites to prove them wrong.

Though the ancient Israelites were recipients of God's miraculous presence, protection, and provision in the wilderness after the exodus, an entire generation died en route to the Promised Land because of their disobedience.

"Don't make the same mistake they did," urges Paul. "Don't turn your liberty into licentiousness! Instead of always thinking of your own personal pleasure, do whatever strengthens the church as a whole" (10:31–11:1).

Orderliness in Worship

From the abuses of Christian liberty (chaps. 8–10), Paul moves into a discussion about the orderliness of Christian worship (chaps. 11–14). He begins with the role of women in the worship service (11:1–16).

Apparently, some women in Corinth "had rejected the concept of subordination within the church (and perhaps in society) and with it any cultural symbol (e.g., a head-covering) which might have been attached to it."[4] Paul reminds the Corinthians, however, that God's design of the man-woman relationship should not be violated in worship. Women and men are equal in Christ (Gal. 3:28), but God has designed their roles to be complementary. One element of that complementary nature is the man's headship, or authority (1 Cor. 11:3).

Once again, Paul is admonishing all members of the Corinthian church to look beyond their own personal needs and do that which builds up the church. In the Lord, "neither is woman independent of man, nor is man independent of woman" (v. 11). And that interdependence should show up in all aspects of church life, including worship.

The Corinthians were even taking the Lord's Supper in a disorderly and disrespectful manner (vv. 17–34). They saw the occasion as an opportunity for gluttony and drunkenness, rather than a reverent remembrance of the Lord and partaking of His goodness. In doing so, they invited God's discipline.

"Satisfy your hunger and thirst at home," Paul exhorts, "so that everyone will have opportunity to partake in this sacred meal" (v. 34).

4. Lowery, "1 Corinthians," p. 529.

So self-centered were the Corinthians, they couldn't even see that the spiritual gifts God had given them were for God's glory, not their own. Paul deals with this abuse in chapters 12–14.

The Corinthians were elevating some spiritual gifts above others, so some members of the church had developed an inflated sense of importance, while others felt inferior. So Paul sets out to explain the concept of the church as the body of Christ (chap. 12).

The Corinthians had missed the whole point of God's giving a variety of gifts in order to unify the body of Christ (vv. 4, 25). All the gifts were important; each one was given to strengthen the church as a whole (v. 7). The Corinthians, though, by worshiping the gift instead of the Giver, were actually dividing the church.

To get them back on track, Paul stresses the importance of each person serving as he or she has been gifted, and seeing all gifts as equally valuable to the body.

What keeps the exercise of spiritual gifts in proper perspective? What allows them to be expressed with equal value and honor? What keeps the gifts from becoming opportunities for self-exaltation? In a word, love—the topic Paul addresses in chapter 13.

As important as the spiritual gifts are to the life of the church, love is more important still. Our greatest activities and accomplishments, exercised without love, are empty and temporal (vv. 1–3). But love does what is right; it seeks the highest good of another. In that way, love has eternal value (vv. 4–13).

> But now faith, hope, love, abide these three; but the greatest of these is love. (v. 13)

Love leads us to seek the edification of the whole church, not just personal satisfaction. So Paul urges the Corinthians to seek the gifts which benefit the entire congregation (chap. 14). Prophesying, for example (v. 1), which most commentators agree is the declaration of God's Word, edifies the body; whereas speaking in tongues mainly edifies the individual exercising that gift (v. 4).

Not that Paul was against speaking in tongues; he gives instructions on how to do it properly (vv. 27–28). He urges, though, that everything in worship must be done without confusion, in an orderly manner (v. 40).

The Resurrection

In chapter 15, Paul addresses the belief of some in Corinth who denied the resurrection of the body. "If Christ has not been raised," he asserts, "then our preaching is in vain, your faith also is vain" (v. 14). Christ's resurrection is not only the assurance of His divine nature but also the hope that we will one day be raised to live with Him forever.

The apostle closes with instructions on collecting funds within the church and sends personal greetings. His final words are appropriate for a man who has so stressed the importance of love in the church: "My love be with you all in Christ Jesus" (16:24).

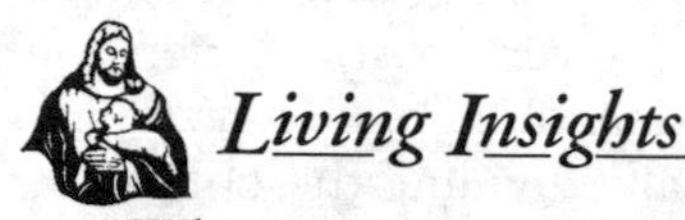

Living Insights

"What's my spiritual gift? Do I have one gift, more than one gift? Do I have the 'most important' gifts? Do I have to be certain about my gifts before I serve?"

Such questions have caused anxiety in many a church member. And church leaders, often unwittingly, contribute to that anxiety. People are exhorted to serve. We're encouraged to "find" our spiritual gifts. "Spiritual gift tests" have been devised to help determine where people should serve. The truth is, it doesn't have to be that complicated.

You want to know where you're gifted? Ask yourself these questions: "What is it that I love to do? What makes me feel like I'm 'in my niche'? Where do I have a lot of experience? What activities do I always seem to gravitate toward when serving on committees and teams? What tasks do I perform that are consistently affirmed and appreciated by others?"

After some honest reflection, you'll probably see a pattern emerge, and you can come pretty close to pinpointing how you can best serve the body of Christ. If people cover their ears and run when you sing, chances are you're not choir material. If you detest details and think whoever invented math should be flogged with a slide rule, you probably wouldn't be happy serving as the church treasurer. And if you would rather be boiled in oil than be with children, don't sign up to run the nursery.

The thing to remember is that you *are* gifted. God has equipped you in a unique way to strengthen and encourage His church. By giving some thought to who you are and how you function, you can find a place of joyful service in the body. And don't be afraid to try out more than one area of service. Finding out what you're *not* good at is a step toward discovering what you do best.

Chapter 9

2 CORINTHIANS: A MAN AND HIS MINISTRY

A Survey of 2 Corinthians

What is this? Another letter to the Corinthians? Were they Paul's favorites or something? Well, he certainly loved them, but that's not why he wrote them another letter. As Eugene Peterson explains,

> The Corinthian Christians gave their founding pastor, Paul, more trouble than all his other churches put together. No sooner did Paul get one problem straightened out in Corinth than three more appeared.[1]

This time, the Corinthians had challenged the authority of Paul's leadership. His first letter, apparently, had hit too close to home. But rather than "argue with what he had written; they simply denied his right to tell them what to do."[2]

What on earth was happening in Corinth?

Background to 2 Corinthians

You would think that 2 Corinthians would pick up where 1 Corinthians left off, like a sequel. However, after the first letter was sent off around the spring of A.D. 55, a number of additional problems arose for Paul with this difficult congregation.

> Paul was in Ephesus when he wrote First Corinthians and expected Timothy to visit Corinth and return to him (1 Cor. 16:10–11). Timothy apparently brought Paul a report of the opposition that had developed against him in Corinth, and Paul made a brief and painful visit to the Corinthians (this visit is not mentioned in Acts, but it can be inferred from

1. Eugene H. Peterson, *The Message: The New Testament in Contemporary English* (Colorado Springs, Colo.: NavPress, 1993), p. 368.

2. Peterson, *The Message*, p. 368.

2 CORINTHIANS

Introduction—Greeting (1:1–2)

	Crucial Concerns	Grace Giving	Apostolic Authority
	Suffering and God's comfort New Covenant ministry Persevering in godliness	Example of Macedonians Command to Corinthians	Reply to critics Justification of ministry False teachers Visions, revelations, credentials, warnings God's power perfected in weakness
	CHAPTERS 1:3–7:16	*CHAPTERS 8–9*	*CHAPTERS 10:1–13:10*
Scope	Past	Present	Future
Issue	Misunderstandings, concerns, explanations	Financial project	Vindication of Paul's ministry
Tone	Forgiving, grateful, bold	Confident	Defensive and strong
Main Theme	Paul's defense of his apostleship and message		
Key Verses	"For we do not preach ourselves but Christ Jesus as Lord." (4:5)	"God loves a cheerful giver." (9:7)	"I will not be put to shame." (10:8)

Conclusion—Farewell (13:11–14)

> 2 Cor. 2:1; 12:14; 13:1–2). Upon returning to Ephesus, Paul regretfully wrote his sorrowful letter to urge the church to discipline the leader of the opposition (2:1–11; 7:8). Titus carried this letter. Paul, anxious to learn the results, went to Troas and then to Macedonia to meet Titus on his return trip (2:12–13; 7:5–16). Paul was greatly relieved by Titus' report that the majority of the Corinthians had repented of their rebelliousness against Paul's apostolic authority. However, a minority opposition still persisted, evidently led by a group of Judaizers (10–13). There in Macedonia Paul wrote Second Corinthians and sent it with Titus and another brother (8:16–24). This took place late in A.D. 56, and the Macedonian city from which it was written may have been Philippi. Paul then made his third trip to Corinth (12:14; 13:1–2; Acts 20:1–3) where he wrote his letter to the Romans.[3]

What tumultuous times Paul endured! Let's sit beside this hard-pressed yet patient apostle and see what was on his heart as he wrote to the beloved, exasperating church in Corinth.

Paul's Style

Second Corinthians is Paul's most emotionally revealing and autobiographical epistle. His humility and great love for these believers shines through nearly every chapter, revealing "the tenderness of a spiritual shepherd sensitive to the needs of his flock (1:24; 2:6, 7; 6:1; 10:2; 13:5, 10) and also the pleading of a spiritual father jealous of his children's affection, purity, and unity (6:11–13; 11:2, 3; 13:11)."[4] But sentimental this letter is not. Paul has some serious issues to contend with, which he addresses candidly—sometimes even with biting sarcasm, especially in chapters 10–13.

This letter is also the least systematic of Paul's writings; rather than following an orderly, logical course, Paul's ideas tend to flow wherever they will. One subject spills into another, and his many

3. Bruce Wilkinson and Kenneth Boa, *Talk Thru the Bible* (Nashville, Tenn.: Thomas Nelson Publishers, 1983), pp. 388–89.

4. Murray J. Harris, "2 Corinthians," in *The Expositor's Bible Commentary*, gen. ed. Frank E. Gaebelein (Grand Rapids, Mich.: Zondervan Publishing House, Regency Reference Library, 1976), vol. 10, pp. 314.

digressions bend the river of his thoughts first this way, then that. Does this mean that his letter is disconnected, disjointed, and haphazard? Not at all. The Holy Spirit, remember, was working through Paul, using his experiences, pain, and reflections to reveal deep reservoirs of truth about Christ.

Reflections of Christ

Second Corinthians reveals just how deeply Paul had been formed in Christ and how clearly he reflected Him. Like Jesus, Paul was not always esteemed by the people he came to minister to, though he shared the Gospel of life (compare Isa. 53:3; John 6:66–68). Both Jesus and Paul had their ministries affirmed by miraculous signs and healing, yet they both were disbelieved. By Christ's "wounds we are healed" (Isa. 53:5 NIV), and by Paul's enduring his wounds and persevering to deliver the truth, we have received Jesus' healing message. Though Jesus was rich, for our sakes He became poor so that His poverty might make us rich (2 Cor. 8:9). And Paul followed in Christ's steps, willing to accept poverty and persecution in order to make others eternally rich with the Good News of Christ (6:4–10).

Structure of Paul's Letter

Paul's letter basically has three sections, which include many theologically rich digressions. In chapters 1–7, Paul explains his conduct and his unique ministry as an apostle. In chapters 8–9, he urges the Corinthians to finish readying their collection for the needy saints in Jerusalem. And in chapters 10–13, Paul strongly vindicates his apostolic authority.

Paul Explains His Conduct and His Apostolic Ministry (Chaps. 1–7)

As we will see in this first division of this letter, all of Paul's life experiences were surrendered to God not just for his own sake but for the benefit of others.

Suffering and Comfort (1:1–11)

After Paul's gracious yet assertive introduction ("Paul, *an apostle* of Christ Jesus *by the will of God*," v. 1, emphasis added), we get a first look at one of his major themes: suffering. This theme is so significant and constant throughout 2 Corinthians that many commentators view this letter as developing Paul's "theology of suffering."

In this section, Paul emphasizes God's compassion, comfort, and deliverance—the power of His very presence—in the midst of suffering. Paul had undergone a terrible time of suffering in Asia, a kind of emotional crucifixion, so that he "despaired even of life" (v. 8). Through this experience, however, he learned not to trust in his own strength but "in God who raises the dead" (v. 9). Here we find another major theme of Paul's: the power of God displayed in human weakness. Through God's power in him, Paul could extend to others who were suffering the comfort and deliverance he had received and in this way also impart hope (vv. 6–7, 10–11).

Paul's Integrity (1:12–2:11)

After the kind and humble words of the previous section, Paul begins to defend himself to the Corinthians in the next. At the root of the problem was Paul's delayed visit, which the Corinthian believers interpreted as a lack of integrity on Paul's part. Paul assures them that both his conduct and his message are determined by God's wholly reliable standards and not the world's ambiguous ones.

His delay in coming, he explains, was for their benefit. He wanted to give them time to grapple with his corrective letter and repent, so that when they were together their visit would not be full of grief but full of joy (1:23–2:4). He always has their best interests at heart, because he loves them. And his urging to forgive a certain person who had caused great problems underscores his concern for their well-being. By accepting this person's repentance, comforting him, and reaffirming their love, they would preserve their Christian unity and close ranks against Satan, denying the evil one entrance into their community.

True Ministers versus False (2:12–3:6)

In 2:12–17, Paul explains that he sees his ministry as spreading "the sweet aroma of the knowledge of" Christ (v. 14). The fragrance of Christ means life, except it smells like death to those who reject life in Him. Setting life and death before people is an astounding task—and humbling. However, the false teachers took it in stride, as those "peddling the word of God," where Paul asserts that his ministry is done in utmost sincerity, in God's sight.

Feeling like he's having to commend himself to the Corinthians again, Paul tells them that *they are* his letters of recommendation.

They (and we) are living letters on whom the Word writes His message, not with ink but with the Spirit, not on tablets of stone but on the human heart (3:1–3; see Jer. 31:31–33). The Spirit makes Paul adequate for the ministry God has given him, unlike the Judaizers, who trust their own self-sufficiency to keep the letter of the Law (2 Cor. 3:4–5).

New Covenant Ministry (3:7–6:2)

From here Paul's thoughts flow naturally to the fading glory of the Old Covenant, to which the Judaizers[5] were trying to submit the Corinthians. The Law, though a glorious provision of God, could only reveal where people came up short but not empower them to overcome their sins. Paul's ministry, however, is rooted in the continually increasing glory of the New Covenant. Christ had fulfilled the Old and ushered in the New, which grants life by His perfect sacrifice and empowers us through the Spirit's transforming work (vv. 7–18).

In contrast to the self-sufficient false teachers, Paul received his ministry by the mercy of God. In light of his high calling, he has lived and spoken only in truth. If people can't or won't accept that, it's because their minds are blinded and not through some fault of Paul's (4:1–6). And Paul doesn't say that in pride but in deepest humility:

> We have this treasure in earthen vessels, so that the surpassing greatness of the power will be of God and not from ourselves. (v. 7)

He displays the frailty of his humanity and the sustaining power of God in verses 8–11, adding that his example is for the spiritual benefit of the Corinthians and the spread of Christ's Gospel (vv. 12–15). Because of the eternal outcome of his sufferings—heavenly glory—he holds onto his hope and longs to be approved by Christ (4:16–5:10).

Thinking of Christ's judgment seat (5:10), Paul turns his attention to the ministry he has been given—that of spreading the reconciling news of the Gospel (vv. 11–21). As Christ has reconciled us to God, so we, as His ambassadors, are to help others become friends of God through Christ (vv. 18–20). And now is the time to act (6:1–2).

5. Judaizers were Jews who believed in Christ but added the requirement of keeping the Mosaic Law for salvation. To become a Christian, they taught one had to be a Jew first.

New Covenant Separateness (6:3–7:1)

The urgency of the message and the awareness of what's at stake bring Paul's thoughts back to the false teachers. First, he commends himself to the Corinthians again through the record of his self-sacrificing service (6:3–10). Then, in light of the testimony of his life (as opposed to the self-serving style of the false teachers), he urges the Corinthians to "open wide" their hearts to him (vv. 11–13). He warns them about becoming unequally yoked with preachers of darkness and following corrupt paths; then he encourages them to remember the promises they've been given and to live a holy life out of reverence for God (6:11–7:1).

A Pastor's Love (7:3–16)

After briefly defending himself again (7:2–3), Paul reaffirms his delight in the challenging church at Corinth:

> I have great confidence in you; I take great pride in you. I am greatly encouraged; in all our troubles my joy knows no bounds. (v. 4 NIV)

Why would he feel this way? Because God comforted Paul in the midst of his sorrow through their love for him (vv. 5–7). Paul also took great joy that the Corinthians' own sorrow (as a result of Paul's corrective letter) led them to repent, restore their relationship with him, and renew their devotion to him (vv. 8–12). Adding to Paul's encouragement was the way they had refreshed Titus. Paul had boasted to Titus about the Corinthians, and they didn't let him down (vv. 13–16).

Paul Encourages Generous Giving (Chaps. 8–9)

As Paul's thoughts turn toward the unfinished collection for the church in Jerusalem, he hopes that the Corinthians won't let him down here either. By way of spurring them on, he cites the generous example of the poverty-stricken church in Macedonia (8:1–8). Then he reveals the deepest reason for giving: Christ's giving to us (v. 9).

Paul follows this challenge with several clarifications. First, he is not giving commands but advice (vv. 8, 10). Second, he is only reiterating their previously communicated willingness to give, not urging them to give more than they have (vv. 10–12). Third, his goal is fair distribution of funds among Christ's followers, not the impoverishment of one for the wealth of another (vv. 13–15). And fourth, they can trust him with their gift (vv. 16–21). Above all, Paul wants the Corinthians to justify his great pride in them before Titus and a "diligent" brother (8:22–9:5).

"God loves a cheerful giver," Paul reassures them, and He amply rewards those who generously care for others (9:6–11). For a greater spiritual reality is at stake: people turn to God in gratitude and praise when their needs are met, and their hearts and prayers go out to those who have shown the abundance of God's grace (vv. 12–14). "Thanks be to God," Paul exclaims, "for His indescribable gift" of grace to us in Christ (v. 15)!

Paul Vindicates His Apostolic Authority (Chaps. 10–13)

From Christ's grace to His "meekness and gentleness," Paul segues to a defense of himself and his ministry (10:1a). He takes on those who have harshly criticized him as being "timid" in person but "bold" from a safe distance (v. 1b NIV). Indeed, when he does come to them, those who have not yet repented had better hope that he doesn't need to be bold with their sins (v. 2). For his weapons are greater than mere physical weapons; they are "divinely powerful" and ready to do what is necessary to complete the Corinthian community's obedience (vv. 3–6).

After affirming the consistency of his character between his letters and his personal presence (vv. 7–11), Paul reemphasizes that his ministry has been appointed by God and that God's standards—not the world's—are his only standards of measurement (vv. 12–18). For he wants to present the Corinthians to Christ as a pure bride, yet he is frustrated at the ease with which they stray from devotion to Him and fawn over so-called "super-apostles" (11:1–6 NIV).

These false teachers evidently compelled the Corinthians to support them, for Paul next has to defend preaching "the gospel of God to [them] without charge" (v. 7)! Paul refused then and refuses now to be a burden, not to slight them but because he loves them and wants to protect them from those who "disguise themselves as servants of righteousness" (vv. 8–15).

Because the false teachers have boasted of their credentials, Paul feels compelled to play the "fool" and boast of his own: being a pure Jew, suffering for the cause of Christ, having a vision from God (11:16–12:6). Twice he reiterates that the only thing he believes worth boasting about is his weakness, because God's "power is perfected in weakness" (12:7–10).

With biting sarcasm, Paul asks the Corinthians to forgive him for not taking their money as the false apostles had (vv. 11–13). That was very tricky of him, he sardonically concludes (vv. 14–16). But then his tone changes, becoming more urgent, pleading, and sincere. He hopes against hope that the sinful ones among them will have repented before he comes so that he won't have to discipline them in the severity his authority as an apostle entitles him to. For he would much rather use that authority "for building up and not for tearing down" (12:17–13:10).

In concluding his long and wide-ranging letter, Paul exhorts this church community he loves to "be made complete, be comforted, be like-minded, live in peace; and the God of love and peace will be with you" (v. 11). His next instruction, "Greet one another with a holy kiss" (v. 12),

> is particularly appropriate to the church in Corinth, whose fragmentation is evident throughout this letter and is reflected in the admonitions of the previous verse.[6]

Then, after conveying greetings from "all the saints" (v. 13), Paul blesses them in the full extent of one called to be an apostle by the Triune God: "The grace of the Lord Jesus Christ, and the love of God, and the fellowship of the Holy Spirit, be with you all" (v. 14).

And may they be with us as well.

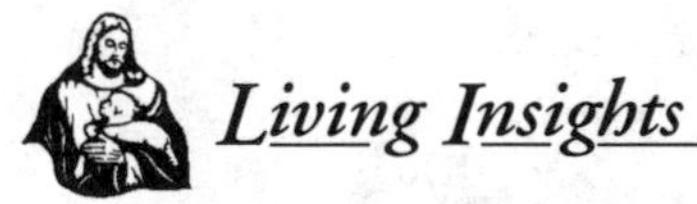

Living Insights

"That's your choice and your responsibility—not mine. If you want to go in that direction, you will bear the consequences. I wash my hands of the whole thing."

How many of us, if we'd been treated by the Corinthians as Paul had, would just get fed up and "let them learn the hard way"?

Thank God Paul did not . . . and thank God that He does not.

Paul kept after the Corinthians because he loved them with a love that wanted their best. Throughout his letter, every hardship,

6. Paul Barnett, *The Second Epistle to the Corinthians* (Grand Rapids, Mich.: William B. Eerdmans Publishing Co., 1997), p. 617.

every sorrow, every comfort, every hope, every scolding, every confidence was for their benefit. Even Paul's defense of himself did not have as the goal simply upholding his own integrity. He wanted them to know the trustworthiness of his character so that they would trust his message and align themselves once again with Christ's truth.

In this way, Paul models God's tenacious love for us. Throughout the Old Testament, He would get frustrated with His people's obstinate waywardness. But He sent miracle after miracle to show His loving care, prophet after prophet to call them back from death to life in Him. Finally, He sent His own Son—all the treasure of heaven incarnate in an earthen vessel. And He keeps after us, like a shepherd searching out a lost sheep, like a woman turning her house upside down for a lost coin (see Luke 15).

Truly, His is a love that will not let us go, and how grateful we are for that.

O Love that will not let me go,
I rest my weary soul in Thee;
I give Thee back the life I owe,
That in Thine ocean depths its flow
May richer, fuller be.

. . . .

O Joy that seekest me thru pain,
I cannot close my heart to Thee;
I trace the rainbow thru the rain,
And feel the promise is not vain
That morn shall tearless be.

. . . .

O Love that will not let me go,
I rest . . . in Thee.[7]

7. George Matheson and Albert L. Peace, "O Love That Will Not Let Me Go," in *The Hymnal for Worship and Celebration* (Waco, Tex.: Word Music, 1986), no. 374.

Chapter 10

GALATIANS: LETTER OF LIBERATION

A Survey of Galatians

Why would a slave, once freed, go back to living in bondage? Why would he willingly place his healed ankles back in the shackles that had scraped them raw? Why would he, having breathed the sweet, pure air of the Gospel and felt the warmth of the Son on his soul, return to the dark, dank dungeon of legalism?

That's what the apostle Paul wanted to know about the Galatians. "I am amazed," he said, "that you are so quickly deserting Him who called you by the grace of Christ, for a different gospel" (1:6). This "different" gospel was no gospel at all—but a message of faith *plus* works. It undermined the real Gospel, making salvation a partially human accomplishment instead of a miraculous and merciful work of God.

So Paul set out to correct this heresy and encourage the Galatians to hold fast to the Gospel he had preached to them—the Good News of freedom in Christ Jesus.

Name and Background

The name "Galatians" is used to designate two different groups of people. Used in a purely ethnic sense, it applies to a people of Celtic descent (Gauls) who settled in northern Asia Minor (modern-day Turkey). The name is also used, however, in a geopolitical sense for the entire Roman province of Galatia, which included the northern region of Asia Minor but extended southward almost to the Mediterranean Sea.

Scholars have debated for years about whether Paul wrote to the people of the "ethnic north" or those living in the southern region of Roman Galatia. The evidence suggests that Paul wrote to the southern Galatians, since his first missionary journey took him to that region—Pisidian Antioch, Iconium, Lystra, and Derbe (see Acts 13:4–14:28). And Paul consistently referred to the churches he had visited in a geopolitical sense.

So the Galatians were most likely inhabitants of southern Galatia who converted to Christianity during Paul's first missionary

GALATIANS

	Personal Words from Paul	Doctrinal Teaching	Practical Exhortations
	Defense of the True Gospel	**Freedom from Legalism**	**Freedom to Love and to Serve**
	"For I would have you know, brethren, that the gospel which was preached by me is not according to man. For I neither received it from man, nor was I taught it, but I received it through a revelation of Jesus Christ." (1:11–12)	"Therefore the Law has become our tutor to lead us to Christ, so that we may be justified by faith. But now that faith has come, we are no longer under a tutor." (3:24–25)	"For you were called to freedom, bethren; only do not turn your freedom into an opportunity for the flesh, but through love serve one another." (5:13)
	CHAPTERS 1–2	*CHAPTERS 3–4*	*CHAPTERS 5–6*
Style	Vigorous, blunt, direct, and brief		
Main Theme	Justification comes by faith in Christ Jesus, not by works of the Law.		
Key Verse	"Nevertheless knowing that a man is not justified by the works of the Law but through faith in Christ Jesus, even we have believed in Christ Jesus, so that we may be justified by faith in Christ and not by the works of the Law; since by the works of the Law no flesh will be justified." (2:16)		

journey. Paul probably wrote to them from Antioch after that journey, around A.D. 49, making Galatians Paul's earliest epistle and one of the oldest New Testament books.

Structure and Style of Galatians

Since Galatians is Paul's response to a specific heresy, the letter is direct, concise, and easy to follow. The first two chapters are *personal*; Paul defends his apostleship and the validity of the Gospel he preaches. Chapters 3 and 4 are more *doctrinal*, focusing on the defense of justification by faith and how it liberates from legalism. The last two chapters get more *practical*, as Paul exhorts the Galatians to live out their Christian freedom in a spirit of love and service.

Personal Words from Paul (Chaps. 1–2)

> Paul, an apostle (not sent from men nor through the agency of man, but through Jesus Christ and God the Father, who raised Him from the dead). (1:1)

Right away, the reader senses that Paul is about to pit the message and authority of God against that of mere humans. And as God's spokesman, he does just that. As we will see, the Galatian letter is about choosing between God's effective and exclusive way of salvation and futile, fabricated formulas.

"Another" Gospel

Paul is amazed that the Galatians have turned to a false gospel (v. 6). And he doesn't hide his disappointment, as commentator Donald K. Campbell explains.

> Conspicuous by its absence is Paul's usual expression of thanksgiving to God for his readers. Instead he vented his astonishment and anger over the Galatians' defection. When compared with the opening of 1 Corinthians this is even more striking, for despite the Corinthians' deep moral defection Paul nonetheless expressed commendation. But here in the face of theological departure

> he did not express thanks, thus emphasizing the more serious nature of doctrinal apostasy.[1]

Paul sees the Galatians' defection as turning not only from a message but from Christ Himself ("deserting Him who called you," v. 6); for the gift of salvation is inextricably linked with its Giver.

Just what was this "other gospel"? Commentator G. Walter Hansen provides some insight on the false teachers' message.

> Not long after Paul planted the churches in Galatia, some Jewish Christians taught these new believers that it was necessary to belong to the Jewish people in order to receive the full blessing of God. Therefore they required the marks of identity peculiar to the Jewish people: circumcision, sabbath observance and kosher food (see 2:12–14; 4:10; 5:2–3; 6:12–13). . . .
>
> The message of the rival teachers struck a responsive chord in the Galatian churches. The Galatian converts may have been feeling a loss of social identity, since their new faith in Christ excluded them from both the pagan temples and the Jewish synagogues. So they sought identification with the Jewish people—God's people—by observing the law. . . .
>
> Their focus shifted from union with Christ by faith and dependence on the Spirit to identification with the Jewish nation and observance of the law.[2]

These teachers—often called Judaizers—thought Paul had gone too far, that his gospel was too easy and advocated loose living. For salvation to be attained and assured, they believed that Jewish ritual and ceremony must accompany faith. In other words, Christ alone wasn't enough.

Paul has a word for the Judaizers: "[They are] to be *accursed!*" (Gal. 1:8–9). The Greek term *anathema* suggests eternal condemnation. Strong words, though not surprising ones, coming from a

1. Donald K. Campbell, "Galatians," in *The Bible Knowledge Commentary*, New Testament edition, ed. John F. Walvoord and Roy B. Zuck (Wheaton, Ill.: Scripture Press Publications, Victor Books, 1983), p. 590.

2. G. Walter Hansen, *Galatians*, The IVP New Testament Commentary Series (Downers Grove, Ill.: InterVarsity Press, 1994), pp. 15–16.

man who had meticulously striven to keep the ceremonial law but found it unable to save him (see 1:14; Phil. 2:4–11).

Christ alone is our salvation, our righteousness. To require human works for salvation is to give ourselves credit for what only He can do.

Paul's Gospel: Directly from Christ

In order to show that his message is indeed the true Gospel, Paul sets out to prove that not only the message but the messenger—Paul himself—was appointed by God.

Paul's assignment to preach the Good News came directly from Jesus Himself (Gal. 1:12). Rather than immediately consulting with the other apostles, Paul spent time alone with God in Arabia developing his theology (v. 17). Though he did associate with other church leaders, Peter and James among them (vv. 18–19), Paul didn't depend on them for his understanding of the Gospel.

Paul isn't diminishing the importance of human teachers here. He's just emphasizing that the Gospel is God's message, not man's. Justification by faith is a product of divine revelation, not earthly fabrication.

Paul's newly found grace was evident in his life as well as in his message. He who had once persecuted the church became her most outspoken champion (vv. 20–24).

That Paul's message didn't come from the apostles, however, didn't mean he was preaching something different. He was no theological maverick; he preached the same Gospel of grace as the other church leaders. For example, Paul had met in Jerusalem with the other leaders to deal with the matter of how Jewish ceremonial law fit into the Gospel message. At that meeting, all the apostles agreed with Paul that circumcision was not a requirement for salvation (2:1–10). Their agreement proved that Paul was preaching the same message they were.

The Destructive Influence of Legalism

But even apostles can buckle under peer pressure. Paul reminds the Galatians that he had to confront Peter, of all people, for drifting into legalism. At the church in Antioch, Peter had disregarded Jewish dietary laws to eat with his Gentile brothers, with whom he was now one in Christ. But when certain Jews came to Antioch, Peter, fearing reproof from the "party of the circumcision" (v. 12), refused to eat with the Gentiles and once again put himself under the Law. His hypocrisy even misled Barnabas (vv. 11–14).

That's the kind of insidious power legalism can have over a person. Peter and Barnabas, both champions of the Gospel of grace, succumbed to those who elevated rule-keeping over redemption. They temporarily slipped back into the shackles of legalism.

But, as Paul also argued in Romans, the Law doesn't make sinners righteous in God's eyes; it doesn't justify them. Only faith in God can do that, because only God can do that (vv. 15–21; see also Rom. 3:21–26).

Doctrinal Teaching (Chaps. 3–4)

Having established that his Gospel is God's Gospel, Paul turns again to the Galatians' defection and draws a sharp distinction between law and grace.

Justified by Faith, Sanctified by Law?

The Galatians' backsliding was "foolish," since they had already responded to the message of Christ's crucifixion (Gal. 3:1). That message not only saves people, it matures them. The Cross is more than a way of escape for the sinner; it's a way of life for the saint. How can we who are saved by grace expect to grow by slipping back into legalism?

The Galatians had received the Spirit by faith, suffered for their faith, and responded in faith to the miracles they had witnessed (vv. 2–5). Having begun by faith, Paul wonders, how could they now depend on their own works?

The Example of Abraham

Not even Abraham, father of the Jews, was saved by works. He "believed God, and it was reckoned to him as righteousness" (v. 6). "Contrary to what the Judaizers taught," says Campbell, "the Law could not justify; it could only condemn."[3] Because anyone who breaks any part of God's Law is under the curse of death (v. 10). Jesus bore that curse and gave us His righteousness so that we could be saved (vv. 11–14).

God's promise of justification by faith, so vividly portrayed in Abraham's life, wasn't nullified by the giving of the Mosaic Law at

3. Campbell, "Galatians," p. 598.

Sinai some four hundred years later (vv. 15–18). Justification has always been by faith. The Law was given to show us God's standards and our sin (v. 19); it served as a tutor to bring us to faith in Christ (v. 24).

Now, as believers, we and the Galatians are part of the family of faith, where neither race, gender, nor social status provide an advantage. We are all corecipients of the grace of God in Christ Jesus (v. 28). We're all "Abraham's descendants, heirs according to promise" (v. 29). We're no longer slaves under the Law but sons and daughters under the grace of God (4:7).

Paul's Personal Plea

In light of the Galatians' new position in Christ, it's easy to see why Paul was dumbfounded that they would abandon all this—why they would "turn back again to the weak and worthless elemental things" (v. 9). They were even using their calendars (the ritualistic observation of "days and months and seasons and years") to gain additional merit before God (v. 10).

Paul pleads with them to "become as I am" (v. 12), that is, free from the Law. They had once before welcomed Paul and his message of freedom (vv. 13–15). But now it's as though the Galatians consider him an enemy—simply because he's telling them the truth (v. 16). Their real enemies, though, are the Judaizers, who want to "shut [the Galatians] out" from hearing the truth (v. 17).

True Children of Abraham

In a brilliant twist of irony and with the sting of sarcasm, Paul turns again to the example of Abraham (vv. 21–31). Since the Galatians "want to be under the law" (v. 21), Paul takes them to one of the Jewish books of Law, Genesis—to show them they are free. They are children of the covenant of promise through Abraham and Sarah, not children of the bondwoman, Hagar (v. 31).

Practical Exhortations (Chaps. 5–6)

Paul has defended both his apostolic authority and the doctrine of justification by faith. Now he turns his attention to a defense of the life of Christian freedom to answer the Judaizers' objections that the Gospel promotes lawlessness and loose living.

"Keep Standing Firm"

Having been set free in Christ, the Galatians are to "keep

standing firm and . . . not be subject again to a yoke of slavery" (5:1). Circumcision, and all ritualistic observances that seek to gain salvation, put Christians back under the Law[4] (vv. 2–3). The Judaizers' insistence on circumcision had hindered the Galatians from growing in Christ (v. 7).

Such teaching is not of God (v. 8). As leaven permeates bread (v. 9), so this teaching permeates the church and obscures the doctrine of grace. Paul is confident that the false teachers will be judged (v. 10). In some of his strongest language, the apostle even wishes the pro-circumcision crowd would fall victim to their own practices and mutilate themselves (v. 12).

Free to Love One Another

No, the Galatians were not set free to fall back under the Law. Neither were they liberated to live licentiously. They were set free to love and serve one another (vv. 13–14), and to display true Christlike character (vv. 22–23). As new creatures in Christ, we are free to love God and love our neighbor. In doing so, we fulfill the intent of the Law.

An individual who is overtaken by sin, though, should be lovingly approached and restored by those stronger in the faith (6:1). By helping others with their spiritual struggles, we "bear one another's burdens" and fulfill Christ's law of love (v. 2). Yet each person is also responsible for bearing his own load as he is able (v. 5).

We also love one another by financially supporting our pastors as we benefit from their ministry and by doing good to all people, especially those within the church (vv. 6–10).

A Final Word

Paul closes with a final rebuke of the false teachers, who want to boast in circumcision instead of the Cross (vv. 12–13). However, he desires to boast only in the "cross of our Lord Jesus Christ" (v. 14). For it is the Savior who died on that cross—not the practice of circumcision—that creates new life (v. 15). And Paul has suffered greatly to preach that message (v. 17).

In closing, Paul leaves the Galatians with what they need most—grace.

4. Paul was not against circumcision, per se. He had Timothy circumcised so that the young man could have a wider ministry among the Jews (see Acts 16:1–3). But Paul detested the teaching that circumcision was a requirement for salvation.

> The grace of our Lord Jesus Christ be with your spirit, brethren. Amen. (v. 18)

Christ has set us free. Let us live free.

Living Insights

Nowadays, insistence on circumcision isn't the chief hindrance to the Gospel of grace. But we're still tempted to view other activities in addition to faith in Christ as essentials for salvation. Baptism, for example. Or being at church every time the doors open. Or abstinence from movies, alcohol, and "secular" music.

While all these are important issues for each Christian to consider, not one of them can be added as a condition for our salvation. Only trusting in Christ—His perfect life, substitutionary death, and victorious resurrection—can save us.

Can you identify any merely human activities in your own life that have found their way into your "salvation essentials"? If yes, list them:

____

____

____

____

Now, how has your study of Galatians helped you to differentiate the true Gospel from a contrived one?

____

____

____

If you catch yourself drifting into legalism, come back to this page. And let freedom ring.

Chapter 11

EPHESIANS: TRUE PORTRAIT OF THE CHURCH

A Survey of Ephesians

In the Corinthian letters, Paul confronted the quarrels that were tearing apart the church. In Galatians, he dueled the legalists who were taking people captive. In Ephesians, however, he steps aside from the conflicts of his day and reveals a magnificent vision of Christ and His grand design for His church. Commentator Walter Liefeld states Paul's purpose this way:

> Paul wrote to expand the horizons of his readers, so that they might understand better the dimensions of God's eternal purpose and grace and come to appreciate the high goals God has for the church.[1]

In this letter, Paul lifts our heads above the smoke and dust of our struggles and gives us a view of what Christ has done for us and why. He gives us a higher perspective, a new vision of our purpose and calling as the body of Christ and how we are to live it out.

In Ephesians, Paul blends some of the loftiest theology in Scripture with some of the most practical teaching. He shows us the deeper reality of God's all-encompassing rule and how our daily, seemingly mundane lives contribute to the accomplishment of His glorious plan.

The Writer and Recipients

Paul wrote Ephesians in Rome around A.D. 61, while he was under house arrest awaiting trial before Caesar (see Acts 25:11–12; 28:30–31). Although guarded by soldiers, he freely welcomed visitors, preached the Gospel, and wrote to the churches. Besides Ephesians, he penned three other epistles during this period: Philippians, Colossians, and Philemon.

To whom did Paul write this letter? "To the saints who are at Ephesus and who are faithful in Christ Jesus" (Eph. 1:1b). By

1. Walter L. Liefeld, introduction to Ephesians, in *The NIV Study Bible*, ed. Kenneth L. Barker and others (Grand Rapids, Mich.: Zondervan Bible Publishers, 1985), p. 1790.

EPHESIANS

	Introduction (1:1–2)	Our Position in Christ	Our Practice on Earth	Conclusion (6:21–24)
		Section 1: What God has done for us (1) Emphasis: Sovereignty Section 2: What Christ has done in us (2:1–10) Emphasis: Grace Section 3: What Christ has done between us (2:11–3:21) Emphasis: Reconciliation *CHAPTERS 1–3*	Section 1: Our new unity (4:1–16) Section 2: Our new walk (4:17–6:9) Section 3: Our new strength (6:10–20) *CHAPTERS 4–6*	
Emphasis		Doctrinal: Vertical relationship with God	Practical: Horizontal relationship with others	
Core Phrase		"He chose us in Him . . ." (1:4)	"Walk in a manner worthy of the calling . . ." (4:1)	
Subjects		Declarations of heavenly truths (God's accomplishments)	Exhortations for earthly living (Christians' assignments)	
Prayers		Paul's prayer for Ephesians (1:15–23); Paul's prayer for the whole church (3:14–21)	Christians' prayers for one another (6:18–20)	
Main Theme		The holy community God is creating and how it is to live out its calling		
Key Verses		1:9–10; 4:1–3		

"saints," Paul means anyone whom God has "set apart" for His use —every ordinary, flesh-and-blood sinner who has been saved by God's grace. These particular saints lived in Ephesus,[2] a prominent port city that was home to one of the Seven Wonders of the World, the famed Temple of Diana (also known as Artemis). During Paul's third missionary journey, he lived there three years, helping establish the church founded by Aquila and Priscilla (see Acts 18:18–19:41; 20:31).

The Theme of Ephesians

The overarching theme of Ephesians is found in 1:9–10: God has purposed "to bring all things in heaven and on earth together under one head, even Christ" (NIV). William Barclay explains: "The key thought of Ephesians is the gathering together of all things in Jesus Christ . . . the realization of the disunity in the universe and the conviction that it can become unity only when everything is united in Christ."[3]

This is lofty theology indeed! Perhaps we need to put it in more everyday language to really grasp the scope of this idea. Eugene Peterson helps us here, explaining that Paul shows

> how Jesus, the Messiah, is eternally and tirelessly bringing everything and everyone together. He also shows us that in addition to having this work done in and for us, we are participants in this most urgent work. Now that we know what is going on, that the energy of reconciliation is the dynamo at the heart of the universe, it is imperative that we join in vigorously and perseveringly, convinced that every detail in our lives contributes (or not) to what Paul describes as God's plan worked out by Christ, "a long-range plan in which everything would be brought together and summed up in him, everything in deepest heaven, everything on planet earth."[4]

2. Some early manuscripts don't contain the words "at Ephesus." It could be that Ephesians was a circular letter meant for all the churches of Asia. That may explain why Paul didn't address a specific church problem or make personal references, as he does in his other letters.

3. William Barclay, *The Letters to the Galatians and Ephesians*, rev. ed., The Daily Study Bible Series (Philadelphia, Pa.: Westminster Press, 1976), p. 66.

4. Eugene H. Peterson, *The Message: The New Testament in Contemporary English* (Colorado Springs, Colo.: NavPress, 1993), p. 401.

The Structure of Ephesians

The structure of this letter follows its theme, which has a "double thesis," as William Barclay notes: "First, Christ is God's instrument of reconciliation. Second, the Church is Christ's instrument of reconciliation."[5] Chapters 1–3, then, show that Christ, through His death, resurrection, and exaltation, has reconciled us to God and united Jew and Gentile into "one body," of which Jesus is the head. This section is *doctrinal*, and it reveals our position in Christ. Chapters 4–6 instruct us in how to live in light of our position—our new identity in Christ. This section is *practical*, explaining our part in accomplishing God's work.

Ephesians has an artistic symmetry not found in any of Paul's other letters. In each half, there are three chapters and three subsections. Three prayers also reinforce this structural balance, coming at the beginning (chap. 1), the middle (chap. 3), and the end (chap. 6). Paul also fashions a triad of sevens: seven spiritual blessings in Christ (chap. 1), seven unities of the body of Christ (chap. 4), and seven pieces of armor (chap. 6).

Overview of Ephesians

Our Unity with Christ (Chaps. 1–3)

What Christ has done for us (chap. 1). In the first chapter, the apostle explores the magnitude of God's eternal purpose by first unveiling what Christ has done for us. In 1:3, he exclaims:

> Blessed be the God and Father of our Lord Jesus Christ, who has blessed us with every spiritual blessing in the heavenly places in Christ.

Through Jesus Christ, God has opened His treasure room and poured the gold of heaven into our hands. Paul tallies our sevenfold spiritual assets in verses 4–14:

1. We have been *chosen* before Creation to be holy and blameless (v. 4)
2. We have been *adopted* as God's children (v. 5)
3. We have been *redeemed* (v. 7a)

5. Barclay, *Galatians and Ephesians*, p. 67.

4. We have been *forgiven* our sins (v. 7b)
5. We have been *made to know* God's eternal plan (vv. 9–10)
6. We have *obtained an inheritance* (v. 11)
7. We have been *sealed* by the Holy Spirit, guaranteeing our inheritance (vv. 13b–14)

How difficult God's sovereign grace is to grasp! Paul knew it, which is why he prayed for his readers. He knew of their faith, which resulted in love for all God's people (vv. 15–16). Still, he wanted them to know God better, understand the hope of His calling, realize the glory of their inheritance, and comprehend God's power for them—the very power of the Resurrection and Ascension (vv. 17–20). With heavenly sight, Paul saw Christ's supremacy over every power that exists. And it is through His church—*His body*—that Jesus manifests His rule over all. Eugene Peterson captures this last idea insightfully:

> The church, you see, is not peripheral to the world; the world is peripheral to the church. The church is Christ's body, in which he speaks and acts, by which he fills everything with his presence.[6]

What Christ has done in us (2:1–10). These saints were not always so blessed, so close, so privileged to work with God. By way of showing the grace of their calling in Christ, Paul reminded them where they (and we) came from: "You were dead in your trespasses and sins" (2:1). But Christ's atoning work on the cross—and God's gracious work through Him alone—changed all that.

> God, being rich in mercy, because of His great love with which He loved us . . . made us alive together with Christ (by grace you have been saved). (vv. 4–5; see also vv. 8–9)

In Christ[7] we have been redeemed, raised, reconciled, and recreated for a new purpose: to be the agency through which God can show the "surpassing riches of His grace" and accomplish the work He has predestined us to do for Him (vv. 7, 10).

6. Peterson, *The Message*, p. 403.

7. "Paul's important phrase 'in Christ' (or its equivalent) appears about thirty-five times, more than in any other New Testament book." Bruce Wilkinson and Kenneth Boa, *Talk Thru the Bible* (Nashville, Tenn.: Thomas Nelson Publishers, 1983), p. 402.

What Christ has done between us (2:11–3:21). Christ has not only reconciled people to God; He has reconciled people to each other. In the balance of chapter 2, Paul explained to his Gentile readers that they "who formerly were far off have been brought near by the blood of Christ" (v. 13). Christ became the bridge of peace, joining God's covenant people, the Jews, with the formerly "unclean" Gentiles in order to create one new body—the church (vv. 11–20). This new community is a living temple; one built not with stone and mortar but with flesh and bone, "a dwelling of God in the Spirit" (vv. 21–22). John Stott heightens our understanding of this new unity.

> Through Christ and in Christ, we are nothing less than God's new society, the single new humanity which He is creating and which includes Jews and Gentiles on equal terms.[8]

Paul next explained his unique role in the forming of this "new society" (3:1–13). As the apostle to the Gentiles, his life's vocation was to reconcile them to God, bringing them into God's *family.* So once again, on his charges' behalf, he prayed—not to "God" but to "Father"—and asked that they might know the power of Christ's Spirit, His indwelling presence, and "the breadth and length and height and depth" of His surpassing love (vv. 14–19). Moved by God's overwhelming graciousness, Paul climaxed his prayer in praise:

> Now to Him who is able to do far more abundantly beyond all that we ask or think, according to the power that works within us, to Him be the glory in the church and in Christ Jesus to all generations forever and ever. Amen. (vv. 20–21)

Our Unity with Each Other (Chaps. 4–6)

Paul's "Amen" led straight to a "Therefore" in chapter 4, as he transitioned from doctrine to application. Verse 1 is the pivot point in his letter:

8. John R. W. Stott, *God's New Society: The Message of Ephesians* (Downers Grove, Ill.: InterVarsity Press, 1979), p. 25.

> Therefore I, the prisoner of the Lord, implore you to walk in a manner worthy of the calling with which you have been called.

Our new unity (4:1–16). In laying the groundwork for the one body of Christ living as one, Paul underscored the need for humility, gentleness, patience, and, above all, love (v. 2). These lead up to his key exhortation in this section: "Make every effort to keep the unity of the Spirit through the bond of peace" (v. 3 NIV). The second set of sevens appears here, emphasizing the completeness of this unity—(1) one body, (2) one Spirit, (3) one hope, (4) one Lord, (5) one faith, (6) one baptism, and (7) one God and Father of all (vv. 4–6).

Though we are *united,* we are not *uniform.* The one God has given us many different spiritual gifts—complementing gifts that work together to build up the body of Christ (vv. 7–12). For our goal is to reach unity in the faith and in the knowledge of Christ, maturing to reflect Him more fully in our lives (v. 13). And this only happens "as each part does its work" (v. 16 NIV), which is Paul's transition thought to his specifically practical section.

Our new walk (4:17–6:9). Unlike the darkened, unsaved Gentiles, who never even had the light that was shone on the Jews, the recipients of Christ's more complete light are to live in righteousness and holiness (4:17–24). We are to live in the truth of our new selves—redeemed and lavishly blessed—and work to build up the body of the redeemed rather than tear it down by our old sinful nature (vv. 25–32). As God has treated us, so we ought to treat one another.

Which brings us to a key thought of this section: "Be imitators of God, as beloved children; and walk in love, just as Christ also loved you and gave Himself up for us, an offering and a sacrifice to God as a fragrant aroma" (5:1–2). How can finite human beings imitate an infinite God? By walking in love (v. 2), by walking in purity (vv. 3–7), by walking in light (vv. 8–14), by walking in wisdom (vv. 15–20), and by walking in mutual submission and deference toward one another (5:21–6:9). All of our relationships, Paul explained, should reflect and attest to Christ's reality. It is through a holy life of caring and mutual humility, rather than the dark divisiveness of self-centeredness, that a unity in Christ will be achieved for all the world to see.

Our new strength (6:10–20). Will the world stand up and applaud God's new spiritual community? Some will be drawn to it, but in general, no. Conflict will come, just as Jesus warned in John 15:18–16:4, because forces beyond the mere human sphere oppose God. They oppose the Light that would expose them for what they really are and do. They oppose Christ's headship because they want to fragment the world and keep it separate from God and His purpose of gathering people to Himself in love.

As Christ's body on earth, then, we must stand our ground—because it is the ground of saving truth. So God has graciously given us His "*full* armor," signified in the seven armaments Paul listed: (1) truth, (2) righteousness, (3) peace with God, (4) faith, (5) salvation, (6) the Spirit, God's own word, and (7) prayer (Eph. 6:10–18). Paul himself was a recipient of satanic opposition; he was an "ambassador in chains"—showing the enmity of the world against God's kingdom. So instead of offering a prayer, as before, he asked for prayer that he would proclaim the Gospel with courage (vv. 19–20).

Conclusion (6:21–24)

Paul ended his letter by comforting his readers' hearts; he would send them his personal messenger, Tychicus, to let them know how he was faring in his imprisonment (vv. 21–22). Then he offered them a benediction, promising grace to those in the body of Christ who would love their Head with a steadfast love:

> Peace be to the brethren, and love with faith, from God the Father and the Lord Jesus Christ. Grace be with all those who love our Lord Jesus Christ with incorruptible love. (vv. 23–24)

Let us walk in the light of His love!

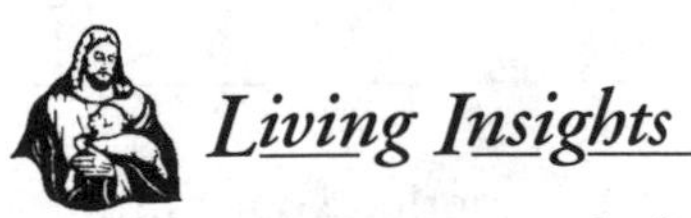

Living Insights

Do you sometimes find it difficult to bridge the gap between what you believe and how you live? Take the subject of unity, for instance. Theologically, we know that all believers are one in Christ. In reality, however, churches divide and Christian families split because people can't get along with each other. Where are the virtues of peace, love, and forgiveness that our faith is built on? Why is it so hard to put them into practice?

Knowing this, Paul did something in Ephesians that will help us more than anything else—he prayed for us. By his example, he showed us how we can pray for ourselves and others we care about.

Take a moment to read his prayers in 1:15–23 and 3:14–21. Briefly summarize what Paul is praying for in both prayers.

What are some common elements in Paul's prayers?

What role does the Father play? The Holy Spirit? The Son?

Putting shoe leather on our beliefs takes more than just human effort. According to Paul's prayers, what does it take?

Has that been missing in your efforts to practice your faith?

As you close this chapter, take a few moments to pray as Paul did for yourself and those you love.

Chapter 12

PHILIPPIANS: JOY IN ABUNDANCE

A Survey of Philippians

Philippians is a book about joy—which is not the same as happiness. On the surface, it's sometimes hard to tell one from the other. An exuberant bride, for instance, may glow with joy or happiness, or both. However, as James Montgomery Boice points out, true joy has its roots in something far more stable than the shifting ground of happiness:

> Happiness is our translation of the Latin word *fortuna*, and it is closely related to chance. Thus, if things happen to work out in a way which we approve, we are happy. If they do not so happen, we are unhappy. Happiness is circumstantial, but not joy. Joy is an inner quality of delight in God, or gladness, and it is meant to spring up within the Christian in a way totally unrelated to the adversities or circumstantial blessings of this life.[1]

That's why we can find joy in some of the unhappiest places—a hospital room, a prison cell, even a cemetery.

How can we tap into that kind of deep-down, abundant joy—the kind that makes our Christianity contagious even during hard times? Is it possible? Paul points us to the answer in his simple yet profound letter of joy written to the Christians in Philippi.

Understanding Some Background Information

If Philippians had been written about happiness, the author would probably have been penning his words while sunning himself on the polished deck of a Mediterranean luxury liner. But since

Portions of this chapter have been adapted from "Your Smile Increases Your Face Value," from the study guide *Laugh Again*, co-authored by Lee Hough, from the Bible-teaching ministry of Charles R. Swindoll (Anaheim, Calif.: Insight for Living, 1992), pp. 1–6.

1. James Montgomery Boice, *Philippians: An Expositional Commentary* (Grand Rapids, Mich.: Zondervan House Publishers, 1971), p. 187.

PHILIPPIANS

	Joy in Living for Christ	Joy in Serving Christ in Unity	Joy in Knowing Christ	Joy in Resting in Christ
	Even when we don't get what we want In spite of circumstances Even with conflicts	Starts with right attitude Maintained through right theology Encouraged by right models	A warning A testimony A goal A command	Unity Peace Contentment
	CHAPTER 1	*CHAPTER 2*	*CHAPTER 3*	*CHAPTER 4*
Christ	. . . my Life	. . . my Model	. . . my Goal	. . . my Contentment
Spirit	His provision (1:19)	His fellowship (2:1)	His worship (3:3)	His peace (4:7)
Positive Reaction	To difficulty: "Now I want you to know, brethren, that my circumstances have turned out for the greater progress of the gospel." (1:12)	To others: "Do all things without grumbling or disputing." (2:14)	To the past: "Forgetting what lies behind and reaching forward to what lies ahead, I press on toward the goal for the prize." (3:13–14)	To the "unchangeables": "Not that I speak from want, for I have learned to be content in whatever circumstances I am." (4:11)
Main Theme	By centering our lives around Christ, we can experience true joy.			
Key Verse	"Rejoice in the Lord always; again I will say, rejoice!" (4:4)			

Philippians is about joy, the circumstances didn't matter. It could have been written from anywhere, even prison.

Who Wrote the Letter?

In fact, Philippians was written by a prisoner—Paul, who was under house arrest in Rome (1:12–14). This was no cushy, TV-and-tennis-courts sentence; he was constantly chained at the wrist to a Roman guard. Even so, nothing could bind the joy Christ had given him for the church at Philippi.

Who Received It?

Paul addressed his letter

> To all the saints in Christ Jesus who are in Philippi, including the overseers and deacons. (1:1)

As to the kind of people they were, Paul gives us some insight with his commendation of their giving.

> You yourselves also know, Philippians, that at the first preaching of the gospel, after I left Macedonia, no church shared with me in the matter of giving and receiving but you alone; for even in Thessalonica you sent a gift more than once for my needs. (4:15–16)

Epaphroditus had just arrived with their most recent financial gift, which Paul called "a fragrant aroma, an acceptable sacrifice, well-pleasing to God" (v. 18).

The Philippians were generous, caring people, most of whom were young in the faith. About a decade had passed since the day Paul first evangelized Philippi, so the leaders in the church were at most ten years old in the Lord. However, their suffering had forced them to mature quickly.

Why Was It Written?

One of the reasons Paul wrote was to encourage them in their suffering. Probably the hostility that Paul endured in Philippi, when he had been beaten and clapped in irons, had turned viciously against them (see Acts 16:16–24). Whatever the nature of their persecution, one thing was sure: it was not in vain. Paul reminded them that they were suffering for Christ's sake (Phil. 1:28–30). He urged them to "stand firm" (4:1; see also 1:27; 2:16) and to "rejoice!"

(2:18; 3:1; 4:4). One day, the Lord would usher them into His kingdom, and they would receive their reward as citizens of heaven (3:20–21).

A second reason for writing was to warn them of predatory enemies who had infiltrated the church: "Beware of the dogs, beware of the evil workers, beware of the false circumcision" (v. 2). Author Lloyd John Ogilvie identifies these vile men as Paul's longtime foes, the Judaizers.

> The Judaizers believed that Jesus was the Savior of Israel only and taught that a person could come to Christ to be saved only through the doors of Judaism. They insisted that all of the legal, ritual, and religious qualifications and demands of the Jews be fulfilled impeccably before a person could grow in Christ. Paul's obvious anger . . . was caused by the way they tried to undo his teaching and ministry. They followed him wherever he went, contradicting his message of justification by faith and the righteousness of God through Christ. And they remained behind after he left a city to confuse the fellowship of grace in the newborn Christians.[2]

Apparently, their mouths were watering over the Philippian believers, and Paul wanted to prepare the believers for future attacks.

Another reason Paul wrote was to strengthen the unity of the church. Rifts among some members were threatening the church's stability. For the Philippians to stand strong, they must stand together. This unity could only be achieved through humility—the kind of humility Christ modeled in his incarnation (2:5–11).

Finally, Paul wrote to warmly thank the Philippians for their financial gift (4:14–18). More than the money, though, Paul particularly appreciated their support at a time when he was feeling the envious jabs of rival preachers in Rome (1:15–17).

The Message of Philippians

Paul wraps all these themes around a central idea: joy in Christ. This buoyant subject rises to the surface on every page of Paul's letter. Sixteen times, he mentions the word *joy* and its derivative

2. Lloyd John Ogilvie, *Let God Love You* (Waco, Tex.: Word Books, 1974), p. 97.

rejoice. But it isn't just joy that Paul has in mind; it is joy in *Christ*. It is the object that makes the joy possible.

Each chapter of Philippians reveals a different facet of Christ. In chapter 1, He is my life; in chapter 2, He is my model; in chapter 3, He is my goal; and in chapter 4, He is my contentment. By centering our lives around Christ, we can experience a joy that transcends our circumstances and spills over into the lives of those around us, bringing unity, love, and hope. That's the message of Philippians.

Survey of the Book

Let's see this message fleshed out as we work our way through the book.

Joy in Living for Christ (Chap. 1)

In the first chapter, Paul illustrates by his own experience in prison how joy in Christ is possible even in difficult circumstances.

He opens by giving thanks for his friends in Philippi, praying for them and reassuring them that God is at work in their lives, just as God has been working in Paul's life, even while he is in prison (1:1–11). Several guards have come to Christ, and the Gospel is spreading through the ranks. Outside prison, unfortunately, some competitors have been preaching Christ "out of selfish ambition," seeking to gain an audience for themselves. Paul could make an issue of it, but he humbles himself (as he will later encourage the Philippians to do) and rejoices that "Christ is proclaimed" (vv. 12–18). His life goal is that "Christ will even now, as always, be exalted in my body, whether by life or by death" (v. 20).

Living for Christ is the secret of joy. Paul writes, "For to me, to live is Christ and to die is gain" (v. 21). With that mind-set, not even the gloom of death can steal our joy because to die is to "be with Christ, [and] that is very much better" (v. 23).

In light of his example, Paul turns to his readers with a challenge: "Only conduct yourselves in a manner worthy of the gospel of Christ" (v. 27a). Like Paul, they have been suffering at the hands of "opponents" (v. 28). And in order to keep their joy, they need to focus on a common goal, "with one mind striving together for the faith of the gospel" (v. 27b).

Joy in Serving Christ in Unity (Chap. 2)

In chapter 2, Paul urges us to find joy in unity with other believers. Two roadblocks, however, are standing in their way: selfishness and grumbling (2:3, 14).

In a powerful statement on Christ's incarnation, Paul shows us the right attitude for getting around those roadblocks: humility. Our Lord perfectly models what it means to set aside one's own interests for the sake of others. He "emptied Himself" (v. 7), or laid aside His divine privileges and became a man. Then "He humbled Himself by becoming obedient to the point of death, even death on a cross" (v. 8). As a result, God has exalted Him, and one day, at His name everyone will bow and confess that He is Lord (vv. 9–11).

We can make Him our Lord now, as we *serve Him in unity*, working out our salvation in tangible deeds of love. Thankfully, we are not left to ourselves in this task, for God is working in us and through us "for His good pleasure" (vv. 12–13). Following Christ's call, Paul has found joy in sacrificing himself for others. He urges us to find the same joy (vv. 16–17).

Timothy and Epaphroditus also model humble servant spirits. Unlike those who seek their own interests, Timothy has proven his worth through his sacrificial work. And so has Epaphroditus, who once "came close to death for the work of Christ" (v. 30).

Joy in Knowing Christ (Chap. 3)

In chapter 3, Paul testifies that the greatest joy in life is knowing Christ because in Him is the righteousness of God that leads to eternal life.

"Rejoice in the Lord"—Paul never tires of declaring this theme (v. 1). The Judaizers, however, rejoice only in themselves. As a former Pharisee, Paul has plenty of reason to glory in his own righteousness like they do. But everything that he once treasured—his name, titles, and trophies—he has tossed on the rubbish heap in order to gain something of much greater value: "knowing Christ Jesus my Lord" (v. 8).

There is joy in *knowing Christ*. To know Him is to believe in Him and receive "the righteousness which comes from God on the basis of faith" (v. 9). To know Him is to experience the death-conquering power of His resurrection in this life and the next. And to know Him is to strive to be like Him in all respects, even if it means suffering and dying as He did. In the end, the prize of eternal life will make it all worthwhile. Until then, we put past mistakes behind us and "press on toward the goal" of knowing Christ, in order to receive the prize that God has waiting for us in eternity (vv. 10–14).

Others may spend their lives seeking earthly pleasures, but "our citizenship is in heaven." We belong to a better place, and we yearn for a greater joy—the joy of being transformed into the likeness of Christ in glory (vv. 19–21).

Joy in Resting in Christ (Chap. 4)

In chapter 4, Paul shows us that to be joyful, we must learn to *rest in Christ*. And a life at rest manifests itself in unity, peace, and contentment.

First is the theme of unity. "Live in harmony in the Lord," Paul tells Euodia and Syntyche (v. 2). Rather than trudge through life nursing grudges and sulking over past hurts, Paul says, "Rejoice in the Lord always; again I will say, rejoice!" (v. 4). Let Him be the One who satisfies your soul, and remember, "the Lord is near" (v. 5b). When He comes, all our conflicts will seem trivial in the light of His glory.

Second, a life at rest is characterized by an inner peace. He writes,

> Be anxious for nothing, but in everything by prayer and supplication with thanksgiving let your requests be made known to God. And the peace of God, which surpasses all comprehension, will guard your hearts and your minds in Christ Jesus. (vv. 6–7)

It focuses on what is true, honorable, right, pure—essentially, the characteristics of Christ. "Practice these things," Paul writes, "and the God of peace will be with you" (vv. 8–9).

Third, it is characterized by contentment, which is something everyone longs for but few people find. He says the secret is depending on Christ in all circumstances: "I can do all things through Him who strengthens me" (v. 13). And he reassures the Philippians that they can depend on Him too, for

> my God will supply all your needs according to His riches in glory in Christ Jesus. (v. 19)

The letter closes with Paul giving glory to God and offering the grace of the Lord Jesus Christ to his readers. *Glory* and *grace*—two words that perfectly summarize the life and ministry of Paul.

So how do we live a life of joy? First, we need the right model, Jesus Christ; second, we need the right attitude, humility; third, we need the right goal, knowing Christ; and fourth, we need the right release, resting in Christ. Christ is the key. He is the light that blazes so brilliantly through the book of Philippians. And He is the gem of joy that shines in our lives.

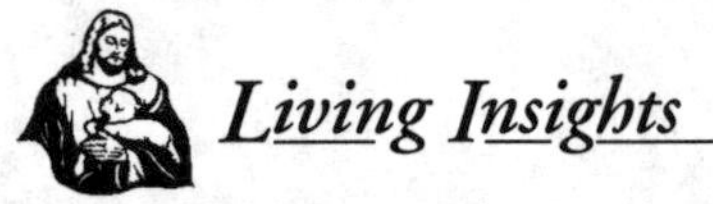

Living Insights

In bold script, the Declaration of Independence states that every human has the right to pursue happiness. And that's what most people do their whole lives—*pursue* happiness. But how many of us actually find it?

Happiness is like sand. One moment we have it in our grasp, and then the weather changes or our mood swings or our fortune turns and whatever happiness we had slips through our fingers.

A better goal is the pursuit of joy. And the only real place to find joy is in Christ. As you think over the main headings in Philippians, which one stands out as a way you can find more joy in your life?

- Joy in living for Christ (chapter 1)
- Joy in serving Christ in unity (chapter 2)
- Joy in knowing Christ (chapter 3)
- Joy in resting in Christ (chapter 4)

Write down a verse from that chapter that you can use to guide your pursuit of joy.

____

____

____

____

Now, that's something you can get your hands around and keep with you the rest of your life.

Chapter 13

COLOSSIANS: CHRIST, OUR ALL IN ALL

A Survey of Colossians

Anyone who has ever searched for the answer to the question, "Who is Jesus?" must eventually come to Colossians. Take a look at a few of Paul's descriptive words about Christ in this book:

- He is the image of the invisible God (1:15)
- By Him all things were created (v. 16)
- In Him all things hold together (v. 17)
- In Him all the fullness of Deity dwells in bodily form (2:9)

Few passages in Scripture present Christ's preeminence more clearly. However, this is only the foundation of Paul's message. Built on that powerful theme is its logical implication: if Christ is *supreme*, then He must be *sufficient* for all our spiritual needs.

If He can create us, then He can redeem us. And, as commentator R. C. Lucas writes,

> If Christ's is the power which sustains the whole universe from remote beginnings to its final goal . . . is it reasonable to doubt His power to sustain the individual believer from conversion to glory? Put in this way it would, of course, be absurd, even monstrous, to deny the adequacy of Christ. But, as we shall see, something like that was happening [in Colosse].[1]

How were the Colossian believers denying the adequacy of Christ? To answer this question, let's first get a little background on the church and the city.

1. R. C. Lucas, *The Message of Colossians and Philemon: Fullness and Freedom*, The Bible Speaks Today series, ed. John R. W. Stott (Downers Grove, Ill.: InterVarsity Press, 1980), p. 47.

COLOSSIANS

	Christ Is Our Lord		. . . Our Life	. . . Our Love
	Lord of creation Lord of the church Lord of ministry	Lord of our walk Lord of our salvation Lord of our growth	Our mind Our body Our attitude Our actions	Love for “outsiders” Love for believers
	CHAPTER 1	*CHAPTER 2*	*CHAPTER 3*	*CHAPTER 4*
Subject	Instruction	Warnings	Exhortations	Reminders
Christ	His person and work		His peace and presence	
Emphasis	Doctrinal and corrective		Practical and reassuring	
Main Theme	Christ is our supreme Lord and sufficient Savior.			
Key Verses	“For in Him all the fullness of Deity dwells in bodily form, and in Him you have been made complete.” (2:9–10a)			

The Church in Colosse

Located about a hundred miles east of Ephesus, Colosse was at one time a wealthy and populous city, situated in the Lycus River valley. When the road system changed, however, Colosse's trade business declined. By Paul's day, the city had been reduced to an insignificant market town. Today "there is not a stone to show where Colosse stood and her site can only be guessed at."[2]

Although small, Colosse was home to a growing church that was founded by a man named Epaphras, probably during Paul's three-year stay in Ephesus. Later, when Paul was under house arrest in Rome, Epaphras came to him with a report that a dangerous new teaching was spreading through the church. At stake was the core doctrine of the Christian faith—the Person of Jesus Christ. Paul wrote Colossians to put a stop to the heresy before it spread out of control.

The Colossian Error

Mixing Christianity with a dash of Jewish legalism and a pound of pagan mythology, the false teachers in Colosse had concocted an odd blend of religions. They taught that faith in Christ wasn't enough. True salvation came through knowledge gained by spiritual enlightenment. Jewish dietary laws, festivals, and rituals (2:16), along with asceticism, astrology, "the worship of angels," and mystical "visions" (v. 18) were among the many rungs on the ladder to enlightenment. A snobbish mentality seeped into the church, dividing the congregation between the spiritual haves and have nots.

Perhaps it was their attempt to introduce Jesus into the intellectual discussions of the day, to make Christianity more palatable, to be "contemporary"—but its effect was essentially to dethrone Christ. As commentator Curtis Vaughn has said, "It gave Christ a place, but not the supreme place."[3]

Combining beliefs in this way is called *syncretism*, and it wasn't just a first-century problem. Christians in every generation have

2. William Barclay, *The Letters to the Philippians, Colossians, and Thessalonians*, The Daily Bible Study Series, rev. ed. (Philadelphia, Pa.: Westminster Press, 1975), p. 92.

3. Curtis Vaughn, "Colossians," *The Expositor's Bible Commentary*, gen. ed. Frank E. Gaebelein (Grand Rapids, Mich.: Zondervan Publishing House, Regency Reference Library, 1978), vol. 11, pp. 166–168.

been tempted to season their theology to the taste of the current culture. The problem is Christ can't be mixed with the philosophies of the world. He stands alone.

Survey of the Book

The book of Colossians divides itself between the doctrinal and the practical, between the truth about Christ and our response to that truth. In the first two chapters, Paul writes eloquently about the supremacy of Christ and the sufficiency of His atonement. Here the emphasis is on *the person and work* of Jesus.

In the final two chapters, Paul fills our sails with the wind of truth he has just revealed and sets us into motion. Just as Jesus empowers His creation, He empowers us in our everyday actions and relationships. Paul's focus here is on *the peace and presence* of Christ.

Christ Is Our Lord (Chaps. 1–2)

To remedy the heresy in Colosse, Paul administers a strong dose of doctrine, summed up in the phrase "Jesus is Lord."

He Is Lord of Creation (1:1–17)

He begins his letter with a greeting (1:1–2), then he offers thanks for the Colossian believers (vv. 3–8). He goes on to pray for them (vv. 9–14), asking the Lord that his readers will walk in a way worthy of Christ,

> to please Him in all respects, bearing fruit in every good work and increasing in the knowledge of God. (v. 10)

That, in a nutshell, is the grand goal of the Christian life. But how do we achieve it? Through the "knowledge of His will," "spiritual wisdom and understanding," and divine strength (vv. 9, 11). All of this God has provided for us, when He "transferred us to the kingdom of His beloved Son, in whom we have redemption, the forgiveness of sins" (vv. 13–14).

In verse 15, Paul uses two significant words to describe Christ: "He is the *image* of the invisible God, the *firstborn* of all creation" (emphasis added). The first word is *eikon* in Greek, which means "manifestation." More than a mirrored reflection, Christ manifests the full nature and being of God. If you've ever wondered what

God was like, all you have to do is look at Christ—the One through whom God revealed Himself to the world.

The second word in Greek is *prototokos*. By saying that Christ is "the firstborn of all creation," he doesn't mean that Christ was the first to be created. *Prototokos* is a title of honor. "The highest honor which creation holds belongs to him," writes William Barclay.[4] The word implies Christ's supremacy over creation, which Paul elaborates in verses 16–17.

> For by Him all things were created, both in the heavens and on earth, visible and invisible, whether thrones or dominions or rulers or authorities—all things have been created through Him and for Him. He is before all things, and in Him all things hold together.

Notice the prepositions: "*by* Him," "*through* Him," "*for* Him," and "*in* Him." Like the Gnostics who came later, the false teachers argued that, because matter is evil, the world was created by an inferior emanation of God. "Not so," says Paul. Christ Himself is the instrument of creation. He is the cause, the mediating agent, the purpose, and the sustaining power.

He Is Lord of the Church (1:18–23)

Christ is also "head of the body, the church" (v. 18). There is no "ladder" of spirit beings through whom we rise to God, as the false teachers claimed. There is only Christ, who was the first to rise from the dead and in whom the "fullness" of God dwells (vv. 18–21).

He Is Lord of Ministry (1:24–29)

The inscrutable truth of the Gospel is this: "Christ in you, the hope of glory" (v. 27). Just think, the One in whom Deity dwells, dwells in us—amazing! Paul's life reverberates with this message, even in his suffering (vv. 24–25). He preaches only one subject: "We proclaim Him" (v. 28a). And his ministry has only one purpose: to "present every man complete in Christ" (v. 28b).

He Is Lord of Our Walk (2:1–7)

The false teachers were trying to convince the Colossians that they are *in*complete because they lacked a deeper knowledge of

4. Barclay, *The Letters to the Philippians, Colossians, and Thessalonians*, p. 119.

God. They couldn't have been more wrong. All believers possess the secret to true knowledge because we have Christ, "in whom are hidden all the treasures of wisdom and knowledge" (v. 3). All we must do is "walk in Him" (v. 6). Spiritual "walking" is the opposite of spiritual "striving." Instead of the emphasis being on our own strength it is on Christ's. We walk *in* Him—in His steps and *in* His power.

He Is Lord of Our Salvation (2:8–15)

Paul further exhorts us not to be taken captive by "philosophy and empty deception" which are based on "the tradition of men" and "the elementary principles of the world" rather than on Christ (v. 8). He draws our eyes back to Christ with three powerful statements in verses 9–11:

- "In Him all the fullness of Deity dwells in bodily form." (v. 9)
- "In Him you have been made complete." (v. 10)
- "In Him you were also circumcised with a circumcision made without hands." (v. 11)

According to the legalists, the Gentiles have to be circumcised before God will accept them. But Christ has already circumcised them spiritually (vv. 11–12). He has forgiven them (vv. 13–14), and He has triumphed over all the forces of evil that might accuse them (v. 15). Their salvation is complete.

He Is Lord of Our Growth (2:16–23)

Because Christ is adequate for every spiritual need, no one has the right to judge believers according to a list of laws and rituals (vv. 16–17). Self-abuse, angel worship, or strict ascetic creeds such as "Do not handle, do not taste, do not touch!" can't move anyone one inch closer to God (vv. 18–22). Paul discards these methods as products of "self-made religion." They "are of no value against fleshly indulgence" (v. 23).

But if those things don't help us battle sin and mature spiritually, what does? Paul answers this question in the remainder of the book.

Christ Is Our Life (3:1–4:1)

Because of all that Paul has said about Christ, and our relationship to Him, our lives should be different. Paul shows how this truth can be applied in four areas.

In Our Minds (3:1–4)

Spiritual maturity begins in the mind, where our priorities and perspectives are formed. Paul tells us to seek "the things above" and set our minds "on the things above" (vv. 1–2). One writer has put it this way: "You must not only *seek* heaven; you must also *think* heaven."[5] Since our lives are "hidden" or secured with Christ (v. 3), we belong to the realm where He is, and we must focus our hopes, desires, and ambitions on that realm. Someday when He returns, our true selves "will be revealed with Him in glory" (v. 4), and we will step into the world of which we've only dreamed.

In Our Bodies (3:5–7)

In verse 5, Paul moves from the mind to the body.

> Consider the members of your earthly body as dead to immorality, impurity, passion, evil desire, and greed, which amounts to idolatry.

God hates sexual sins. One day, His wrath will boil over on those who have rejected Christ in favor of their lusts (v. 6). Paul's command is very strong here: if we want to grow in Christ, we must take God's point of view concerning immoral practices and "put them to death."

In Our Attitudes (3:8–17)

Next, he addresses our attitudes. Like clothes, some attitudes belong to the wardrobe of the "old self": anger, wrath, malice, slander, abusive speech, lying. Paul says to toss those rags aside because, when God united us with Christ, He updated our style. He has given us new clothes to wear—compassion, kindness, humility, gentleness, patience, forbearance, forgiveness, and the golden crown of love (vv. 12–14). When we put on these attitudes, our lives are adorned with unity, peace, and joyous songs (vv. 15–16).

In verse 17, Paul sums up what it means to live in Christ.

> Whatever you do in word or deed, do all in the name of the Lord Jesus, giving thanks through Him to God the Father.

5. Lightfoot, as quoted by Curtis Vaughn, "Colossians," p. 209.

In Our Relationships (3:18–4:1)

Paul also touches on our family roles: wives are to submit to the leadership of their husbands; husbands are to love their wives; children are to obey their parents; fathers are not to exasperate their children (vv. 18–21). "Slaves," or employees, are to work as if they are working "for the Lord rather than for men" (v. 23), and "masters" (bosses) are to treat their slaves with fairness, "knowing that you too have a Master in heaven" (4:1).

Christ Is Our Love (4:2–18)

In the final chapter, Paul asks his readers to devote themselves to prayer and encourages them to be wise in their dealings with outsiders (vv. 2–5). Sprinkle a little grace on your words, Paul says (v. 6). Then he concludes his letter with a section of personal words about his fellow workers (vv. 7–18).

A Final Thought

Like the mast on a sailing ship, the theme of Christ rises high and occupies the center place in Colossians. Every aspect of our faith, from our salvation to our sanctification to our glorification, is tied to this center pole.

Would you say that Christ is the center of your life? Do you seek Him when you sense a spiritual need? Or do you turn to books, seminars, or emotional experiences? Certainly those things aren't wrong in themselves, but if they take Christ's place, we can lose our spiritual equilibrium like the Colossians did. Paul's message to them and to us is clear: Christ alone is sufficient for all our spiritual needs.

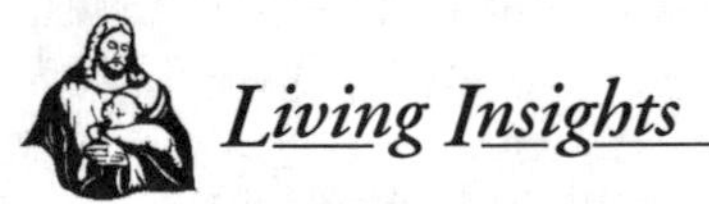

Living Insights

It takes just one wrong turn to get a person lost. The Colossian believers made their wrong turn when they bought the lie that Christ wasn't enough to make their lives complete. That mistake got them side-tracked into some crazy ideas about spirituality: self-abuse, worshiping angels, celebrating the new moon.

What happened to the Colossians can happen to us too. It begins with a nagging doubt that maybe God left something out of our salvation. Perhaps we need a new list of rules to live by or an ecstatic experience to take us to the next level.

Have you ever thought that something was missing in your spiritual life? If so, what doubts haunted your mind? __________

____

____

Paul had to lead the Colossian believers back to the place they made their wrong turn, reassuring them, "In Him you have been made complete" (2:10). Then he pointed them in the right direction, "Therefore as you have received Christ Jesus the Lord, so walk in *Him*" (v. 6, emphasis added)—not all these other things.

What does it mean for you to walk in Christ with reference to your mind (see 3:1–4)?______________________________

____

____

Your body (see vv. 5–7)? ______________________________

____

____

Your attitudes (see vv. 8–17)? __________________________

____

____

Your relationships (see 3:18–4:1)?______________________

____

____

How can you tell whether you're taking the wrong turn? Ask yourself, "Is this path leading me to Christ?" If so, keep going. You can be sure that you're heading in the right direction.

Chapter 14

1 THESSALONIANS: A HEART-TO-HEART TALK

A Survey of 1 Thessalonians

Paul. Renowned apostle. Brilliant theologian. Commanding orator. Prolific writer. Concerned parent.

Concerned parent? We usually don't put Paul in the "parent" category; after all, he was a bachelor. Yet, in a spiritual sense, he was father and mother to hundreds, even thousands of God's children scattered throughout the Mediterranean world. To Paul, each conversion under his ministry was like the birth of a baby. And each new church was like a nursery, full of the joy and challenges of new life.

Concern for the young churches weighed heavily on his mind. Like a traveling father who ached for his children back home, Paul yearned to be with his new converts—to make sure they were getting the proper spiritual nourishment, to protect them from lurking strangers like the Judaizers, to soothe their fears, to guide them through difficult decisions, to prepare them for the future.

The two letters Paul wrote to the Thessalonians are full of parental affection and advice. With the tenderness of a mother's touch, he affirmed and encouraged them in their growth. And with the strength of a father's voice, he answered their theological questions and corrected their moral waywardness.

As we open the first of Paul's letters to this church, let's go back to the beginning of his relationship with them, to the day he first arrived at the bustling port city of Thessalonica.

Background of the Book

Entering Thessalonica, Paul would immediately have been impressed with its size. Situated at the crossroads of two major trade routes, it was the largest city in Macedonia and the capital of its province. This diverse center of commerce represented a golden opportunity for Christianity, a potential hub out of which the Gospel could travel to all points of the Roman Empire.

Paul began his ministry there in the synagogue. For three Sabbaths, he preached the Good News of Jesus Christ; and several Jews

1 THESSALONIANS

	The Pastor's Heart . . .			The Pastor's Burden . . .	
	Thanksgiving Remembering Affirming Reporting	The pastor among the flock The flock's response to the pastor	Personal concern Comfort and relief	Sexual purity Prophetic urgency	Stay alert! Encourage one another! Live in peace!
	CHAPTER 1	*CHAPTER 2*	*CHAPTER 3*	*CHAPTER 4*	*CHAPTER 5*
Perspective	Looking back			Looking ahead	
Subject	The church itself	The apostle himself	The report	The concern	The balance
Especially Appropriate For . . .	. . . new converts	. . . young pastors	. . . suffering Christians	. . . tempted and uninformed Christians	. . . "sleepy" Christians
Main Theme	The hope of Christ's return comforts us and motivates us to godly living.				
Key Verses	1:8–10; 4:1, 13–18				

believed, as well as many Greeks who had turned to Judaism to find God.

Some Jews from the synagogue, however, were jealous of Paul's influence, so they formed a mob and incited the city against him. Paul was forced out of town, leaving the new believers in a vulnerable position. They were only a month or two old in the Lord. Would their newborn faith survive the persecution? Would the Jews lure them away from Christ? Would they weaken under temptation and revert to their former ways?

From Thessalonica, Paul went to Berea and eventually to Athens. In Athens, he couldn't stand not knowing any longer how the Thessalonians were faring, so he sent Timothy "to strengthen and encourage" them and "find out about [their] faith" (1 Thess. 3:2, 5).

Paul then moved on to Corinth, where he waited anxiously for word from Timothy. Finally, the young assistant arrived with his report. Much to Paul's relief, the news was good: Their faith in Christ had held fast, they were loving one another, and their affection for him was still strong (3:6).

But a few matters still required his attention.

1. He needed to respond to some personal accusations. Evidently, outsiders were trying to dishearten the believers by questioning his motives and criticizing him for failing to return.
2. He needed to affirm the young believers in their growth and encourage them to "excel still more" (4:1, 10), particularly in the realms of sexual purity, respect for authority, and church unity.
3. He needed to clarify what he had taught them about the coming of Christ. Some wanted to know what happened to the believers who died before His return. Would they miss going to heaven?

So, around A.D. 50, Paul sat down to write his first letter to the Thessalonians, which some Bible scholars believe was his first New Testament epistle.[1]

Major Theme of the Book

Among the many subjects Paul addresses, the coming of Christ

1. Other scholars believe Galatians was Paul's first epistle, dating it around A.D. 48, between his first and second missionary journeys.

stands out as his major theme. Structurally, it is the framework upon which Paul builds his letter (each chapter ends with a reference to this glorious event). And spiritually, it is the focal point of life that gives us hope and moral direction. Notice the different ways Paul describes Jesus' appearing:

- It rescues us from God's judgment (1:10)
- It is the time for glory, reward, and joy—especially over those we brought to Christ (2:19)
- It is the motivation for holy living (3:13)
- It is the hope and comfort for those in grief (4:13–18)
- It is the goal of sanctification (5:23)

For the Thessalonians, Christ's return was a future reality to help them handle their present problems. For us, it is the same — the one thing we can count on in our uncertain times.

Survey of the Book

We can divide the book into two broad sections. In chapters 1–3 Paul *looks back*. Thumbing through his mental photo album, he traces the history of his visit to Thessalonica and encourages the believers in how much they have grown. In chapters 4–5 he *looks forward*. He exhorts his readers to grow even more in certain areas and addresses some of their questions.

The Pastor's Heart (Chaps. 1–3)

Paul devotes the main portion of his letter to pouring out his heart to his readers.

God's Work Remembered (Chap. 1)

He begins by thanking the Lord for how willingly the Thessalonians embraced the Gospel. Truly, God was at work in their lives, for it wasn't Paul's preaching that turned them around; it was the convicting power of the Holy Spirit (vv. 1–6).

So dramatic was their conversion that the news of it had spread into the surrounding regions. Everywhere Paul traveled, people told *him* how the Thessalonians had turned from worshiping idols and how they were giving their lives to two purposes: "to serve a living and true God" and "to wait for His Son from heaven" (1:9, 10).

Accusations Answered (Chap. 2)

As Paul thinks back on his ministry in Thessalonica, he can't help remembering his critics. They have painted him as a deceitful, self-glorifying people-pleaser who uses converts for personal gain. In response, Paul counters with the truth. His suffering proves that he is not in ministry for himself. His goal in life is to please God, who entrusted him with the Gospel and who knows the true motives of his heart (2:1–6).

If the Thessalonians need further proof of his sincerity, they should recall how gently he treated them, like a mother caring for her babies; and how he exhorted them, like a father encouraging his children. He even took side jobs to pay his own way, giving up many of his rights as an apostle. And all in order to teach them how to "walk in a manner worthy of the God who calls [them]" (v. 12).

Paul truly has their best interests at heart—in stark contrast to their "own countrymen," who were like the Jews who persecuted the church in Judea. Paul comes down hard on these Jews, seeing them and their kind as those who killed Jesus and now hinder him from speaking salvation to the Gentiles. But they're not the only ones blocking his ministry; Satan himself has been keeping him from returning to Thessalonica (vv. 13–20).

Concern Expressed (Chap. 3)

Since Paul could not come in person, he sent Timothy to find out how the believers were doing and to encourage them. Timothy's good report was like a breath of life-giving air to Paul. Nothing gave him more joy than knowing that his converts were standing firm in the Lord (3:1–8).

With a full heart, he prays on behalf of his spiritual children that they will love each other even more in the days ahead and that God will make them holy and pure for Jesus' return (vv. 9–13).

The Pastor's Burden (Chaps. 4–5)

Further developing the themes of love and personal holiness, Paul instructs his readers in two specific areas of their Christian walk: their sexual purity and their relationships (4:1–12; 5:12–28). In the middle of these two themes he answers some questions about what happens to believers after death and at the end of the world (4:13–5:11)—showing the practical outworking of our hope in Christ.

Sexual Purity and Love (4:1–12)

Paul's instructions in this section flow out of his general exhortation in 4:1, "to walk and please God." Pleasing God—not ourselves or other people—is the ethical foundation upon which all moral standards are built. This is also the basis for Paul's command in verse 3:

> For this is the will of God, your sanctification; that is, that you abstain from sexual immorality.

Those who don't know God have no reason to control their lusts (v. 5). But we know God, and He has called us for a unique purpose: *sanctification*.

That word appears three times in this section (vv. 3, 4, 7), and it means "the state of being made holy."[2] God has given us His Holy Spirit to make us holy, but when we sin sexually, we hinder God's sanctifying process in our lives. We reject His holy purpose for us, and in effect, we reject Him (vv. 7–8; compare 1 Cor. 6:12–20).

Having admonished his readers to control their sexual passions, Paul urges them to genuinely love one another—which, practically speaking, means treating others with respect and taking personal responsibility (1 Thess. 4:9–12).

The Coming of Christ and the Day of the Lord (4:13–5:11)

At first, this section on future things feels like a quick left turn in the letter. However, as we saw in our "Major Themes" section, Paul has actually been leading us straight to this subject.

The Coming of Christ (4:13–18). The first event on the timeline is the coming of Christ, which commentator John Stott explains in four key words based on this passage: "the Return, the Resurrection, the Rapture, and the Reunion."[3] Any moment, Christ will suddenly appear, raise the bodies of believers who have died, rapture or "snatch up" living believers (instantly glorifying their bodies), and reunite the living and the dead with Himself "so we shall always be with the Lord" (v. 17).

For Christians, this means that death is not good-bye. We may

2. Walter Bauer, *A Greek-English Lexicon of the New Testament*, trans. William F. Arndt and F. Wilbur Gingrich, 2d ed., rev. (Chicago, Ill.: University of Chicago Press, 1979), p. 9.

3. John R. W. Stott, *The Message of 1 and 2 Thessalonians*, The Bible Speaks Today Series (Downers Grove, Ill.: InterVarsity Press, 1991), p. 105.

grieve the passing of a loved one, but we do not grieve "as do the rest who have no hope" (v. 14). At the Rapture, we'll have the greatest reunion party this world has ever known!

The Day of the Lord (5:1–11). Unfortunately, the trumpet blast that announces the rescue of believers will also signal the doom of unbelievers. Christ's appearing will set in motion a period of judgment known as "the day of the Lord," and no one on earth will escape its terrors (vv. 2–3).

Thankfully, "God has not destined us for wrath, but for obtaining salvation through our Lord Jesus Christ" (v. 9). As a result, we can encourage each other to live, not like those in the darkness who are under God's judgment, but as people of light (vv. 4–8, 11).

Living in the Light (5:12–28)

How do "light" people live? Paul sketches a practical picture in verses 12–22. In their relationships, they

- Appreciate and esteem their leaders (v. 12–13a)
- Live in peace (v. 13b)
- Admonish, encourage, help, and show patience to each other (v. 14)
- Don't retaliate but seek good for others (v. 15)

And in their walk with the Lord, they

- Rejoice, pray, give thanks (vv. 16–18)
- Don't quench the Spirit or despise prophetic ministry (vv. 19–20)
- Abstain from every form of evil (v. 22)

Paul sums up the message of his letter in a beautiful benediction:

> Now may the God of peace Himself sanctify you entirely; and may your spirit and soul and body be preserved complete, without blame at the coming of our Lord Jesus Christ. Faithful is He who calls you, and He also will bring it to pass. (vv. 23–24)

To that, we say a thankful "Amen!"

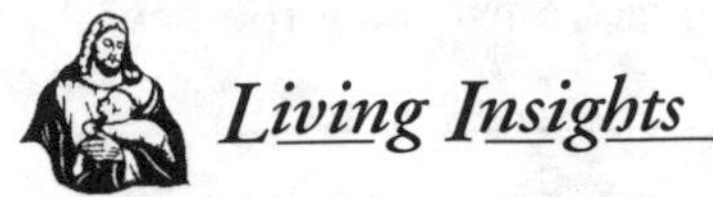

Living Insights

Eugene Peterson, in *The Message*, describes the central role the future plays in our daily life.

> The way we conceive the future sculpts the present, gives contour and tone to nearly every action and thought through the day. If our sense of future is weak, we live listlessly. Much emotional and mental illness and most suicides occur among men and women who feel that they "have no future."
>
> The Christian faith has always been characterized by a strong and focused sense of future, with belief in the Second Coming of Jesus as the most distinctive detail. . . .
>
> The practical effect of this belief is to charge each moment of the present with hope. For if the future is dominated by the coming again of Jesus, there is little room left on the screen for projecting our anxieties and fantasies. It takes the clutter out of our lives. We're far more free to respond spontaneously to the freedom of God.[4]

Do you sometimes feel like you "have no future"? Does your soul need a fresh infusion of hope? Do you want to remove the "clutter" of worry from your life?

For a few moments, lift your eyes from the earthly grind and gaze into your heavenly future. Let the truth of Christ's coming dominate your "screen."

Which of your anxieties fade to insignificance in the light of Christ's return?

____

____

____

4. Eugene H. Peterson, *The Message: The New Testament in Contemporary English* (Colorado Springs, Colo.: NavPress, 1993), p. 428.

What confidence does His return give you to face the day?

____

____

____

What seems more important now than ever before?

____

____

____

We may live and work in the darkness of this world, but we don't belong here. As children of light, we belong to the day. Any moment heaven's light will flood the sky, and the night will give way to a new and glorious dawn. So, as you put your hand to the tasks of everyday living, keep your eyes on the horizon. Keep your heart pure and full of hope. And keep your mind fixed on Christ . . . because He is coming soon!

Books for Probing Further

It's wonderful to attend a symphony, but it's even better to immerse yourself in it. Now that you've completed the fourth major movement of *God's Masterwork*, would you like to give the first half of the New Testament a deeper, longer listen? Would you like to linger more over some of the eternal melodies you've heard? Then the following materials will help tune your ear to their songs. And don't forget, we're holding your seat for the grand finale—the fifth and final volume of *God's Masterwork*. Don't miss it!

Commentaries (in Biblical Order)

Barclay, William. *The Gospel of Matthew.* Rev. ed. 2 vols. The Daily Study Bible Series. Philadelphia, Pa.: Westminster Press, 1975.

Boice, James Montgomery. *The Sermon on the Mount: An Exposition.* Grand Rapids, Mich.: Zondervan Publishing House, Ministry Resources Library, 1972.

English, Donald. *The Message of Mark: The Mystery of Faith.* The Bible Speaks Today Series. Downers Grove, Ill.: InterVarsity Press, 1992.

Wilcock, Michael. *The Message of Luke: The Saviour of the World.* The Bible Speaks Today Series. Downers Grove, Ill.: InterVarsity Press, 1979.

Morris, Leon. *The Gospel According to John.* Rev. ed. The New International Commentary on the New Testament Series. Grand Rapids, Mich.: William B. Eerdmans Publishing Co., 1995.

Stott, John. *The Spirit, the Church, and the World: The Message of Acts.* Downers Grove, Ill.: InterVarsity Press, 1990.

Luther, Martin. *Commentary on Romans.* Trans. J. Theodore Mueller. 1954. Reprint, Grand Rapids, Mich.: Kregel Publications, 1976. The classic work on Romans.

Stott, John. *Romans: God's* Good News *for the World*. Downers Grove, Ill: InterVarsity Press, 1994.

Prior, David. *The Message of 1 Corinthians: Life in the Local Church*. The Bible Speaks Today Series. Downers Grove, Ill.: InterVarsity Press, 1985.

Barnett, Paul. *The Second Epistle to the Corinthians*. The New International Commentary on the New Testament. Grand Rapids, Mich.: William B. Eerdmans Publishing Co., 1997.

Hansen, G. Walter. *Galatians*. The IVP New Testament Commentary Series. Downers Grove, Ill.: InterVarsity Press, 1994.

Barclay, William. *The Letters to the Galatians and Ephesians*. Rev. ed. The Daily Study Bible Series. Philadelphia, Pa.: Westminster Press, 1976.

Stott, John. *God's New Society: The Message of Ephesians*. The Bible Speaks Today Series. Downers Grove, Ill.: InterVarsity Press, 1979.

Boice, James Montgomery. *Philippians: An Expositional Commentary*. Grand Rapids, Mich.: Zondervan Publishing House, 1971.

Lucas, R. C. *The Message of Colossians and Philemon: Fullness and Freedom*. The Bible Speaks Today Series. Downers Grove, Ill.: InterVarsity Press, 1980.

Stott, John. *The Gospel and the End of Time: The Message of 1 and 2 Thessalonians*. Downers Grove, Ill.: InterVarsity Press, 1991.

Gaebelein, Frank E., gen. ed. *The Expositor's Bible Commentary*. Vols. 8–11. Grand Rapids, Mich.: Zondervan Publishing House, Regency Reference Library, 1976–84. These volumes cover Matthew through Philemon.

Walvoord, John F., and Roy B. Zuck, eds. *The Bible Knowledge Commentary*. New Testament ed. Wheaton, Ill.: Scripture Press Publications, Victor Books, 1983.

Other Helpful Books

Colson, Charles, with Ellen Santilli Vaughn. *The Body: Being Light in the Darkness*. Dallas, Tex.: Word Publishing, 1992.

Conyers, A. J. *The End: What Jesus* Really *Said about the Last Things*. Downers Grove, Ill.: InterVarsity Press, 1995.

Edersheim, Alfred. *The Life and Times of Jesus the Messiah*. 1971. Reprint, Grand Rapids, Mich.: William B. Eerdmans Publishing Co., 1986.

Green, Joel B. *How to Read the Gospels and Acts*. Downers Grove, Ill.: InterVarsity Press, 1987.

Pentecost, J. Dwight. *The Words and Works of Jesus Christ: A Study of the Life of Christ*. Grand Rapids, Mich.: Zondervan Publishing House, Academie Books, 1981.

Pollock, John. *The Apostle: A Life of Paul*. Wheaton, Ill.: Scripture Press Publications, Victor Books, 1985.

Swindoll, Charles R. *Laugh Again*. Dallas, Tex.: Word Publishing, 1991.

———. *Simple Faith*. Dallas, Tex.: Word Publishing, 1991.

Wilkinson, Bruce, and Kenneth Boa. *Talk Thru the Bible*. Nashville, Tenn.: Thomas Nelson Publishers, 1983.

Yancey, Philip. *The Jesus I Never Knew*. Grand Rapids, Mich.: Zondervan Publishing House, 1995.

Insight for Living also has study guides available on the Sermon on the Mount, Luke, John, Acts, Romans, 1 and 2 Corinthians, Galatians, Philippians, and 1 Thessalonians. For more information, see the ordering instructions that follow and contact the office that serves you.

Some of the books listed may be out of print and available only through a library. For those currently available, please contact your local Christian bookstore. Books by Charles R. Swindoll may be obtained through Insight for Living, as well as some books by other authors. Just call the IFL office that serves you.

Ordering Information

God's Masterwork

Volume Four

If you would like to order additional study guides, purchase the cassette series that accompanies this guide, or request our product catalogs, please contact the office that serves you.

United States and International locations:

Insight for Living
Post Office Box 69000
Anaheim, CA 92817-0900

1-800-772-8888, 24 hours a day, 7 days a week
(714) 575-5000, 8:00 A.M. to 4:30 P.M., Pacific time, Monday to Friday

Canada:

Insight for Living Ministries
Post Office Box 2510
Vancouver, BC, Canada V6B 3W7

1-800-663-7639, 24 hours a day, 7 days a week

Australia:

Insight for Living, Inc.
General Post Office Box 2823 EE
Melbourne, VIC 3001, Australia

(03) 9877-4277, 8:00 A.M. to 5:00 P.M., Monday to Friday

World Wide Web:

www.insight.org

Study Guide Subscription Program

Study guide subscriptions are available. Please call or write the office nearest you to find out how you can receive our study guides on a regular basis.